Archangel Book of Days

A Year of Daily
Inspiration and Blessings

Archangel Book of Days

A Year of Daily Inspiration and Blessings

Diana Henderson

All rights reserved. No part of this book may be reproduced, stored, or transmitted by any means, whether auditory, graphic, mechanical, or electronic without written permission of both publisher and author, except in the case of brief excerpts used in critical articles and reviews. Unauthorized reproduction of any part of this work is illegal and is punishable by law.
Copyright © 2024 Diana Henderson

ISBN: 978-1-944662-87-5

Publishing date: June 2024

Cover Design and Front Cover graphic
by Diana Henderson © 2024

Dedication

To all the angels in my life who have lifted me when I faltered and stood by me through life's challenges

Acknowledgments

An abundance of thanks goes to Drew Becker, my husband, who has supported my writing and editing work for decades and who is my finest critic. Drew also serves as my editor and publisher.

Thank you to Worth Dewey Henderson, my late father, for being the consummate storyteller and for loving me from the moment I was born. I offer most profound gratitude to Doris Jarrett Henderson, my mother, for awakening and encouraging my love of books and writing and for being a shining light for me and so many others. At 95, she continues to serve the divine and is a living example of love in action.

I send much gratitude to the friends and family who have loved me and who have been my angels in human form by offering kindness, support, and wise counsel.

Thank you to the members of the Order of Archangel Michael and A Gathering of Angels who attended my angel meetings for many years and who believe in the grace of those unseen helpers in our lives.

Introduction

In these fast-paced, often tumultuous times, I've encountered many people who feel overwhelmed and who struggle to navigate the often murky, turbulent waters of our modern age. Sometimes, we all need a buoy or a beacon as life's storms pummel our psyches and currents of fear threaten to overtake our senses.

Daily inspiration can come from many sources. Over the years, I have developed a deep association with Creator's messengers and helpers, the angels and archangels. They serve as powerful allies, offering us a helping hand, a kind presence, loving guidance, and a refuge in times of turmoil. I have experienced angelic intervention many times in my life and likely would not be here without the assistance of the invisible realms.

This book contains daily messages from the archangels that are intended to illumine the path, provide an anchor in the storm, and shift our perceptions toward the light. These messages, which came to me in meditation while communing with the divine, are meant to strengthen your connection to the Creator, to your own spirit, and to the angelic realm.

The bulk of this book consists of those inspirations, one for each day throughout the year. The final section of the book contains meditations and exercises to deepen your relationship with the divine and the angels. Most of these come from classes I have taught for many years. In 2001, I felt called to create the Order of Archangel Michael, which began in June 2002 and continued for many years. In addition, I founded a group dedicated to exploring topics related to angels in December 2005 and held monthly meetings for over 17 years.

Countless times during this journey, I have welcomed angelic aid and guidance. I believe wholeheartedly the Creator sends these messengers to usher us through life's difficult passages and to help steer us toward love, peace, and blessings. We have the choice to heed divine wisdom and follow the path of grace or to stray farther from the home of the heart and soul. I confess I have wandered many, many times away from the truth of my spirit. I am thankful that God's angels remained nearby to lead me safely to harbor every single time.

Please be aware that many of the archangels go by more than one name, depending on religion or culture. Those listed here are simply the names I associate with each of them.

Archangel Michael

The leader of the heavenly host, known as "the great captain," serves as the protector and the warrior against the forces of darkness. Michael ("perfect one of God") and his angelic legions can aid us when we feel lost or in need of a guardian. He also helps us defeat the shadow aspects in our lives, align with divine will, and serve our purpose. When we lack courage or faith, Michael stands with us to support us and remind us of the strength of the spirit.

Archangel Jophiel

Jophiel or Joviel ("beauty of God") and his legions expand divine wisdom, grace, and joy into the world. He helps us get in touch with our inner child and use our imagination to inspire and uplift. He aids in bringing beauty to life through words and art. Those who seek to enlighten, inform, and illuminate through their creative efforts may feel a close kinship to Jophiel.

Archangel Chamuel

Chamuel ("one who seeks God") expands love, compassion, and the beauty of the heart into this world. This beloved archangel invites all to align with the highest law of love. Chamuel awakens the desire to give aid and to create and appreciate beauty. The nurturing essence of a mother's unconditional love flows through Chamuel's heart. His light is soft, gentle, and encouraging.

Archangel Gabriel

Gabriel's name means "God has shown Himself mightily." He is the bringer of glad tidings, the divine messenger, the archangel of annunciation who came to Mary to announce the birth of Jesus. Gabriel is said to sit at the left hand of the Creator. He sounds the horn of hope and serves to awaken all to the divine dream for our lives, to purify the pathways of thought, and to guide us through conflict into harmony. He also serves as a being of creation and manifestation.

Archangel Raphael

Archangel Raphael's name means "God heals" or "God has healed." He is also the archangel of service, divine knowledge, marriage, and the season of spring. His energy is youthful and vibrant, and his light is rejuvenating. Some believe he was the angel who stirred the waters of the healing pool at Bethesda. "For an angel went down at a certain time into the pool and stirred up the water; then whoever stepped in first, after the stirring of the water, was made well of whatever disease he had." (John 5:4)

Archangel Uriel

Uriel's name means "flame of God," "radiance of God," or "light of God." In *Paradise Lost*, Milton referred to him as "regent of the sun." His service to the Creator involves holding the light of peace for all, stimulating devotion to and recognition of the divine, and helping us transcend limiting patterns and issues. He helps us find the light within ourselves in those moments when we feel lost or overwhelmed and reignites the desire to live life to its fullest and dedicate ourselves to the path we came to walk.

Archangel Zadkiel

Zadkiel, whose name means "righteousness of God," aids us in opening to and offering forgiveness and mercy, cleansing thoughts, words, and energies that are out of alignment with peace, grace, and freedom, rising into a higher frequency of love, and liberating our souls and beings of that which limits our connection to the divine.

* * *

Various belief systems designate specific angels or archangels to the days of the week. The angels assigned to each day in this work may differ from those you know.

Sunday: Archangel Michael
Monday: Archangel Jophiel
Tuesday: Archangel Chamuel
Wednesday: Archangel Gabriel
Thursday: Archangel Raphael
Friday: Archangel Uriel
Saturday: Archangel Zadkiel

Week 1

Sunday: Archangel Michael

Faith rises from your heart and beckons you to lift your eyes unto the Light. What you see in the world around you is colored by your inner vision. When you look through the eyes of love and live in the essence of faith, you begin to change your world. Creation's heart calls you to take a leap of faith, to honor the call of your spirit, and step now towards the world you seek to experience.

Monday: Archangel Jophiel

No matter your age or life experience, deep within you lives the child of light you were born to be. Today find a moment to remember that child you once were, to tenderly hold that beautiful being, and remind yourself of the bright, wondrous light you truly are. It is time to laugh and sing and imagine. Bring some measure of joy into your every activity. Your inner child will thank you.

Tuesday: Archangel Chamuel

Kindness can rule the world if you let it. Love paves the way to compassion, peace, and benevolent creation. Love's splendor far outshines the brightest star or the most prized work of art. Let the beauty of your spirit, the unique light Creator gave you, emanate from your heart to wash your corner of the world in gentler hues. In the face of unkindness, speak, "I am love. I abide in love." Look within and you will find it always waiting for you.

Wednesday: Archangel Gabriel

Every moment, the light of creation breathes through you. To fulfill the promise of your spirit, build your reality from the heart. Your bricks and mortar are no less than the essence of Creator's own love, light, and life force. Your tools are the vision you hold, the belief in your dreams, the words you speak, the actions you take, and the thoughts you think. Hands and heart together, held in the embrace of Spirit, give birth to your hopes.

Thursday: Archangel Raphael

Healing comes in many forms. What loving light can you bring into the world today? Will your genuine smile touch another's heart? Will your kind words lift some fellow traveler from the brink? Today, look for the small opportunities to bless another soul and sense the infusion of blessings that flows to you in return.

Friday: Archangel Uriel

Peace abides in the heart and spirit of all who seek it. No matter the turmoil of the world around you, look within your heart and call on the light of your spirit to access this grace. Once you anchor within that light, hold it as long as you can and expand it into your space. The way is clear.

Saturday: Archangel Zadkiel

When you forgive, you lighten the load you carry. Each degree of forgiveness eases your burdens and lifts your own heart. Forgiveness is a divine act that any child of light may perform. Sink into your heart space, tap into the flow and the power of boundless love, and claim your right to forgive deeply and completely.

Week 2

Sunday: Archangel Michael

Today, instead of taking action in the outer world, sit in stillness, where the Divine may speak to your heart. In these moments of silence, of quiet contemplation, listen to the song of your soul. Beyond the mind chatter, the worldly dissonance, and those passing thoughts, the voice of knowing awaits your deepest listening. If you need help to reach that inner space of grace, call upon the Light to still all except the one resounding expression of clarity.

Monday: Archangel Jophiel

What within you needs to be illumined? What weighs upon your heart and mind? Bring it out into the open. Express it in writing or speak it to the Eternal, to the Creator of all. There is an answer to every question, a solution to each problem, a way forward beyond any struggle. Call upon the golden-white light of the Divine Mind to wash away all except the true core of your issue so that you may see clearly what you seek. Then open your being to the solution, the answer, the wisdom of the Infinite Mind.

Tuesday: Archangel Chamuel

Lean into love today. Begin this day by anchoring love in your heart and expanding it from the sacred heart space into the mind. Let love saturate your being as much as you can. The more you practice this, the more easily you will attune to the channel of love divine. Color your world in love's essence, and behold how it shifts your reality. Finally, end the day by showering in the light of love. Let it wash away your worries and clear from your being all that is less than its own essence.

Wednesday: Archangel Gabriel

Wherever you discern conflict, within or without, you may discover the path to harmony. View words of disagreement or unsettling feelings as a means of seeking understanding. Listen with love. Step back from engagement in any frequency of fear and recognize the deeper meaning beyond discord. Commonality exists and common ground may be found when viewing every situation that arises as an opportunity to empathize, comprehend, and more fully come to know another's heart (or your own).

Thursday: Archangel Raphael

To live in clarity means to be free of judgment and filled with love for all. The Divine invites you to clear your mind of those perceptions and beliefs that place anyone (including yourself) beneath their full potential. Let the many frequencies of divine love free you from that which seeks to limit your journey into light.

Friday: Archangel Uriel

What is a miracle except a moment of experiencing God's reality? Seek those moments when your human eyes may behold the truth of the Infinite. You have the power to shape your reality, to align with the frequency of miracles. Lift yourself beyond the mundane. Notice the small miracles that occur when you pay attention to them and to the Light. Focus your awareness on the synchronicities and the subtle shifts toward a higher perception. As you do so, more miracle moments will unfold.

Saturday: Archangel Zadkiel

In human perception, change is often feared. From divine perspective, transformation welcomes blessings. What small or large aspect of your life can you alter today to welcome an influx of beneficial energy? Will you begin to journal? Will you join a mindfulness class? Will you create something to brighten your world? Perhaps you may move the location of pictures on your walls, rearrange furniture, clean out a closet, or tend to some other seemingly ordinary aspect of your environment. Be assured there are no mundane facets of life. Every small shift on the physical level offers some measure of renewal. Honor the need to shift energy and gain a fresh perspective or perhaps even an unexpected blessing.

Week 3

Sunday: Archangel Michael

Your purpose is as unique as your perfect light, born in the heart and mind of the Creator. Are you living that role as fully as you might? Nothing else brings as much gratification as leaning in to your purpose. As you move through your day and your week, notice what draws you, where your strengths lie, and what brings joy into your being. Call on the Divine to guide you in the direction of your truth.

Monday: Archangel Jophiel

When you ask for direction, recognize that your truest guide is ever close at hand. Eternal wisdom lives in your sacred heart space and in the light of your spirit. It is easy to be drawn to the clamor of the world, yet the Creator of all speaks always within the stillness of your innermost being. As often as possible, set aside a few moments of respite from daily life to breathe with the Divine, quiet the noise of the outer world, and listen with your heart to the Divine Mind.

Tuesday: Archangel Chamuel

Today, put on your rose-colored glasses that allow you to see yourself and those around you through the eyes of love. In so doing, you may find your view shifts considerably. You may begin to see beauty everywhere—in those eyes you behold in the mirror, in the aspect of those you love, in the faces of passing strangers, and in the world of nature. The divine artist, the Creator of all, perceives the perfect beauty in every soul. Look with divine love, and you will see the same.

Wednesday: Archangel Gabriel

Your spirit and the Light of the Divine speak ceaselessly to you. Divine messages come in many forms—a fleeting bit of conversation that lingers in your thoughts, a song lyric that draws your notice, a recommendation given to you multiple times, a series of seeming coincidences. Heed the signs along your pathway.

Thursday: Archangel Raphael

The answer lies within your heart, the truest path of healing. Love without attachment. Live without judgment. Bless all without reservation or condition. And rise above the fear that plagues the small self, for fear has no power beyond what you give it. The shadow is nothing when the Light spreads its radiance as surely as the sun.

Friday: Archangel Uriel

Give comfort to your fellow travelers through life as the opportunity arises. A tender smile, a loving embrace, a word of kindness, a helping hand—these gifts earnestly offered have the power to alter the course of a life. Feel the joy that expands in your own heart as you provide such gestures to those who need your aid. Such joy is the great gift of every angel, and you are acting as angels on Earth when you share in this way.

Saturday: Archangel Zadkiel

As you awaken gently from sleep or in those fleeting instants before you fall into slumber, you may find yourself amid the ethereal essence of perfect calm. Pause, breathe, and extend that feeling for as long as you can. Watch for the wonders in waking life as well. Transcendent moments may occur at unexpected times. Embrace them, for they are signs of the eternal.

Week 4

Sunday Archangel Michael

How often have you lost track of time while occupied in a meaningful pursuit? Step outside of time for a span today. Let the persistent construct of time slip away as you enter into a higher level of existence through meditation or deep prayer, a walk in nature, an artistic endeavor—whatever your heart and spirit call you to do. The Divine shines in many activities that draw your attention away from the clock. Experience the divine, timeless moment where angels dwell.

Monday: Archangel Jophiel

Grace lives within you beneath the sea of conscious thoughts and behind the chatter and bustle of the world. Pause for a span beneath the sun. Let its light bathe your being. Tap into the eternal. A radiance far brighter than Sol lives within your soul and anchors in your heart. Renew yourself in that golden-white light.

Tuesday: Archangel Chamuel

Every child of light carries emotional wounds from the experiences of this life. Within your heart lives a frequency of love that has the power to heal those wounds. Imagine yourself sinking into that sacred heart space, calling forth the pink light of love, and allowing that pure essence to encompass and fill you. Let the soothing, gentle waters of love wash through your heart and expand throughout your mind and body. Sense this nurturing energy that feels like a mother's unconditional love. Intend that your wounds of the heart be healed and cleansed by this nourishing light. When you bring your awareness back into the mind, welcome a softer, more loving resonance to color your perceptions.

Wednesday: Archangel Gabriel

At the opening of the day, surround yourself with protective white luminosity. At the close of the day, purify the consciousness and being of all dissonant energies. Wash in the liquid light stream of white and golden-white radiance pouring forth from the Creator of all. Envision this light showering your consciousness, coursing through your body and throughout your space. This practice will serve you well.

Thursday: Archangel Raphael

Each leaf in the Tree of Life holds a truth that can lead to wholeness. Balance and harmony flow through the heart path and guide you to the realm of beauty. Awaken the healer within and recognize that miracles abound. Every experience has led you to this moment. Embrace them all, love them all, acknowledge the knowledge that was born of every breath.

Friday: Archangel Uriel

Angels exist in the pure place of peace outside time, where all things are possible. Breathe divine light and know that you shall manifest this day as you ground the light in this moment. Choose, if you will, to radiate your spirit's light in each moment, and you will discover your highest path.

Saturday: Archangel Zadkiel

Decree the light of Creator's cleansing flame as follows to clear your path this day and cleanse your being at the day's end.

I invoke the Violet Flame
Consecrated in God's Holy Name.
Complete transcendence now I claim.
Transmute all in Violet Flame!
I invoke the Violet Flame
In blesséd Creator's Holy Name.
Ascension's Light I proclaim.
Bathe me now in Violet Flame!

Week 5

Sunday: Archangel Michael

You are made of the stuff of stars and are no less beautiful and bright. Amid the tumult of human existence, you sometimes lose sight of this truth. Journey within and seek the core of your essence within the sacred heart light. The power, compassion, and wisdom of love await you within that space of pure grace. The Divine spark lives forever within your spirit. Seek now that truth.

Monday: Archangel Jophiel

What wonders may spark and come to life within a child's imagination! Recognize, dear soul, that no matter your age, you are a child of light. Creative vision is one of the greatest gifts you came into this world to use. Daydream the world you seek. Take flights of fancy to the places you wish to travel in the physical world. Imagine the glorious blessings you will receive when you open the path to them through a mind innocently accepting of a higher reality. A child fantasizes and believes. It's time for you to do the same.

Tuesday: Archangel Chamuel

Among the universal truths, the highest law is and ever shall be love. Many fluctuations occur within the universe, yet Creator's Love remains constant. From that Love, all blessings flow. To honor the cause of love without judgment or qualification is to live divinely. Your quest today and, in truth, every day is to love every life you encounter—human, animal, plant, and mineral—as the Creator loves you. See how long you can sustain this feeling. The feeling in and of itself is a blessing, yet be assured, in giving love without reservation, divine blessings shall flow to you.

Wednesday: Archangel Gabriel

Communication with Creation's Heart is key to building your dreams. Write your desires on two separate sheets of paper. Craft each one carefully to fully express what you seek. Be sure to include "or greater still" and "according to the highest good and divine will" at the end of your list. Then, speak those hopes to the Creator while holding love, joy, and gratitude in your heart. After you have expressed your dreams to the Divine, burn the first piece of paper, giving to God every one of those aspirations. Once a week for seven weeks, choose one item from your list to include in your bedtime prayers, and ask for a divine dream to guide you on the path to bringing this to fruition.

Thursday: Archangel Raphael

Today, be receptive to the wonders and blessings the Creator reveals to you. The Divine always provides a gift to those who offer light and love from the heart. For all the graces you have given, receive now those little and large miracles you seek.

Friday: Archangel Uriel

As the sun glorifies the morning sky, rise and let your spirit sing the light of divine consciousness. You came to shift this world and shine your own soul's light so that others might know and see the glory of the Creator expressed through you. Remember this truth, and in every moment let it guide your words, thoughts, and emotions, for in each moment you radiate energy. May it always be the light of your true divine essence.

Saturday: Archangel Zadkiel

Rise beyond the mundane today. Let the "real world" pause for a span as you seek the eternal. Raise your awareness to the heights. Allow your consciousness to climb as if it had wings to the highest peaks of your spirit. Just imagine yourself lifting above the fray, seeking the sweet solace of the soul. Look for the luminosity of your spirit and recognize that you can become one with that truth by journeying upward into light. When your mind descends once again into the physical aspect of being, remember that you still have the power to transcend in a matter of moments through inner vision, intention, prayer, and breath. Your consciousness always could.

Week 6

Sunday: Archangel Michael

The angels honor each step you take toward the Light. Whether you progress on the path to enlightenment at a brisk pace or with a slow and steady stride, the Divine walks beside you, celebrating each victory and offering a helping hand each time you falter. Advancement requires intention, determination, and courage. These qualities exist in abundance within the Divine Heart. Set your intentions today and call on the aid of the angelic realm. Trust that you do not walk alone.

Monday: Archangel Jophiel

Your mind is a powerful tool that can be used for good or ill. Learn to observe your thoughts in the moment. Rather than judging stray thoughts, become aware of them and relinquish those that no longer serve you to Creator's cleansing energies. Formulate beneficial patterns by focusing and repeating the thoughts that elicit joy, peace, and harmony. Immerse the mind in the golden-white light of the Divine Mind. Engrave upon the mind the sweet gifts of love, kindness, laughter, and delight.

Tuesday: Archangel Chamuel

At the core of every life lies the desire to be loved. When this love is not provided at the level necessary for true nourishment, the craving deepens and at times distorts into undesirable forms. What seems out of balance in the world often results from a profound lack of love. What can you do? First, look within yourself for those wounds you experienced from an absence of love and call upon divine love to fill your being and heal the traumas of your life. When you have done so to the extent you require in the moment, expand your own heart's sacred song of love until you are ready to honor the need for love within others, even those who seem most at odds with the very gift they fervently seek.

Wednesday: Archangel Gabriel

You are stirring from the deep slumber to the beauty of your powerful light. Beloved child, arise from shadows into the service of the Creator of Harmony, the Regent of Love. Let your heart abound with the sweet song of pure hope that you may share with others this glorious gift. If you feel you have lost hope, then bathe in the golden-white grace that flows forever from the sacred fountain. You are meant to inspire hope, to kindle kindness, and to awaken wonder. Find the spark that remains within your heart, and light the way forward.

Thursday: Archangel Raphael

The Creator invites you to heal the heart. Become one with Creation's Heart. Allow the light of divine love, wisdom, and power to guide your actions and cleanse your being. Release the wounds you have held for your family and for your world. Carrying those wounds no longer serves you or the Light. Welcome release and healing with each step you take toward shedding the hurts of the past.

Friday: Archangel Uriel

Passionately sing your spirit's sweet song as it is given to you by the Creator. Energize that soul truth daily as you connect to the light of peace and begin to live the ideals you were born to expand into the world. Realize you have come with profound purpose to this blessed Earth at this time so that your unique soul song, uniting with the chorus of light workers, teachers, and angels, would build the crescendo in the great symphony of light that will usher this planet into a finer age.

Saturday: Archangel Zadkiel

You may perceive freedom in many ways, but it has never depended on the actions of others or the circumstances in which you find yourself. A prisoner in the deepest dungeon may consider him or herself free when in touch with the truth of the spirit. A human surrounded by luxury and opportunity may remain bound to the chains of fear and its imprisonment of the self. Recognize that liberty exists as the certainty of the spirit. Find your freedom by altering any mindset of fear that confines you.

Week 7

Sunday: Archangel Michael

When you feel adrift and unanchored, trust that guidance shall come. Call upon the divine power that flows through all life, including your own being, to illuminate the path before you. Access your inner knowing, and, in faith, follow the wisdom that is given as you focus intently upon the Light.

Monday: Archangel Jophiel

Accept the silken sweetness flowing forth from Creation's Heart. Allow yourself to bathe in a honey soft illumination as gentle as sunlight. If you have held yourself apart from comfort, separated yourself from the one true Source of blessings, open your heart to them now.

Tuesday: Archangel Chamuel

At the core of Creation's Heart, Creator beckons you to embrace creativity, love, and harmony. Love yourself as the Divine loves you, and then share that blessed gift with all who cross your path. Live as an emissary of light and harmony. As you choose to align with the divine heart of creation, you can make great strides in shifting to a higher level in any aspect of life. Anchor this loving light and embrace a resonance that encourages blessings.

Wednesday: Archangel Gabriel

Warm as the light of the sun, you touch each hand and heart with love. Yours is the gift of luminescence that ignites awakening and lights the way to peace. Sweet and soft is the light of the Divine Mother, whose pure song is sung in your soul. Leave the mind behind on occasion as the heart aligns your eternal spirit.

Thursday: Archangel Raphael

Gratitude expands the heart and opens the pathways of blessing from the eternal wellspring of Creation. When gratitude extends from the heart into the mind, nothing less than Love can live in your consciousness. Let the sunlight of the divine grace fill you to overflowing and all good things will unfold before you.

Friday: Archangel Uriel

Where are you on the journey of transformation? Consider the caterpillar on its journey to become a butterfly. The butterfly begins as a caterpillar crawling on the earth. In its larval phase, the caterpillar sheds its skin repeatedly in order to grow. As a pupa, the caterpillar disassembles and reassembles its cells to become at last a butterfly. Emerging, this new life form strengthens its wings and prepares to fly. Are you ready to find your wings? The Light stands with you as a patient witness to your transcendence.

Saturday: Archangel Zadkiel

The growing pains that surface as old patterns fall away must be released into love. Entrust yourself to a higher power. Bathe in the light of forgiveness. Give your own heart and life the empathy you offer to others.

Week 8

Sunday: Archangel Michael

Many think of angels as your champions in the realms of light. Recognize that you are Creator's champions in the realm of Earth, and it is through the combined efforts of humanity and the Divine that all shall rise and awaken to higher consciousness.

Monday: Archangel Jophiel

Are you hanging on to patterns or circumstances that have out served their purpose? Are you clinging to something that weighs down your wings? You have the power to shift any pattern in the light, to release the residue of what was and align with the wisdom of what shall be. Are you ready to take a step forward into a future where you shine instead of shrinking from your brilliant light? The angels celebrate each time you allow the glorious luster of your soul to radiate into this world.

Tuesday: Archangel Chamuel

When all is in balance, giving and receiving flow in a perfect circle. The Creator withholds nothing from any soul and endlessly expresses an outpouring of love, life, abundance, and blessings. You are invited to step into the river of light flowing from the eternal fountain. Receive that nurturing energy as surely as you give it. It is time to open to the tide of love and abundance.

Wednesday: Archangel Gabriel

Ask yourself how you may rebirth a higher vision for your own life and for your world. The intertwining of all forms of life allows each soul to affect the greater whole. Therefore, what you choose today influences all others tomorrow. You, child of light, transform the world with your every thought and action. Your inner rebirth can resurrect a higher reality for this world.

Thursday: Archangel Raphael

Empaths process emotional energies for many. Do so with conscious intent. Align yourself today and each day with devotion to the Light. Recognize that you are a healer of light as surely as those who shine within the higher realms. You are the love, light, and beauty of your spirit. Live in that knowing.

Friday: Archangel Uriel

In all of creation, there is no other like you. As you shine your unique, divinely created essence, you illuminate the world as only you can. Your spirit is needed here to touch other souls and help them remember their own light.

Saturday: Archangel Zadkiel

True freedom occurs when the mind becomes liberated from fear-based patterns and discord. How much are you willing to shift your mindset away from fear and toward love, peace, and wisdom? Rises into a mental construct that is more aligned with spirit requires focus, awareness, and mindfulness. Allow the violet light of Creator to help you clear mental detritus and awaken to a finer reality.

Week 9

Sunday: Archangel Michael

Think, speak, and live consciously. Be ever aware of the energies within and around you. Realize your creative power and live according to divine laws. In the dance of creation, surrender to the Light and what flows forth can be only of that light.

Monday: Archangel Jophiel

You are more than a vehicle for earthly interaction. Your body is a glorious gift, but your consciousness holds far more wonder. Even the human mind at its most powerful pales in comparison to the eternal spirit. Call to your higher self, your spirit mind, your timeless truth, to walk with you today, to lift you into a more transcendent perception that you may recognize the everlasting miracle of your life and of every marvel of the world around you. Appreciate it all from the perspective of Spirit.

Tuesday: Archangel Chamuel

Each morning before you face another day, connect to your inner heart light. Breathe consciously, calling on the soothing, harmonizing essence of the Creator. Blessings in, worries out. Imagine that with every inhale you are drawing in the sweetest, kindest, most loving light in all the universe, for indeed you are. This process occurs naturally when all aspects of consciousness align with Love Eternal. If your concerns impede upon your thoughts, simply intend they be surrendered to Spirit. They will someday melt and evaporate anyway if you let them. Breathe love today and know blessings.

Wednesday: Archangel Gabriel

Like all life on this beautiful planet, you journey among the stars in the sacred dance of the cosmic song. Day-to-day experiences may draw the attention away from this larger vision. When you gaze at the night sky, you become aware of the infinite. The light of the moon and stars immerses you in the remembrance of your true being. Breathe in the infinite. Reach for the stars. Awaken to a higher vision.

Thursday: Archangel Raphael

Healing leads you to expansion of the heart light, and in oneness with that light, you may access abundant blessings. Become as the beloved tree rooted in the Earth and supported by her life force, reaching out to touch all life with grace, stretching ever upward to embrace the heavens. In this way, balanced between heaven and earth, the abundant life force of God flows from above and below and enriches through your breath, your body, your heart, your soul!

Friday: Archangel Uriel

Set aside a time to surrender to the stillness, to sink softly into the silence. Sense the oneness and embrace the sweetness that comes when you pause from daily life and commune with the Divine. Sunrise and sunset are optimal times to connect to the peace of Creator. Give yourself this experience as often as you can. Your life may be calmer for it.

Saturday: Archangel Zadkiel

You recognize that the angels exist in a state of complete oneness with Creator and with all life, yet in this physical aspect of life, you may have forgotten that you do as well. Each of God's creations is a unique expression of the eternal and infinite One. The idea of separation from the whole is mere illusion. When you align with higher consciousness, you become more aware of that oneness and begin to realize the seeming boundaries perceived in this matter-based reality are nothing more than a misapprehension. Within the infinite sea of the eternal, each drop of water holds the power of the ocean of oneness, and no single drop ever stands alone. Today, as you move through the world, remember you are the ocean and so are all of your fellow travelers. Ask yourself, am I ready to turn the tide toward love and blessings for all?

Week 10

Sunday: Archangel Michael

The bridge to enlightenment awaits you along the pathway of love. The heavenly host beckons you to deepen your daily connection to Creator's love and light so that the veil of shadow may be lifted and all may envision the way to wisdom and glory.

Monday: Archangel Jophiel

Even the simplest things can bring pure joy to a young child. Little ones often display amazing enthusiasm for whatever stands in front of them. They may become engaged and enthralled by a stone, a tree, a favorite toy, a story, or a rhyme. Once something captures their attention, small children exist in a state of wonder and joy. Approach this day as if you were a child encountering each marvel along your route as a new wonder to be explored. Give your attention and interest to those who cross your path. Greet each experience with the heart and perception of a child finding a little miracle along the way. You may find yourself feeling lighter, brighter, and more blessed than you have in a long while.

Tuesday: Archangel Chamuel

Once, long ago in the innocence of childhood, you experienced hurt for the first time. In that moment, a small piece (or perhaps even a large one) of your innocence was taken from you. Before that, you knew you were small in stature as all children are, but you still recognized you were large in spirit. Little by little, year after year, you grew larger in body but perhaps somehow smaller in your own perceptions. The angels watch as these shifts occur in each child of light and desire always to shelter each one from the wounds of the world. Whatever injuries your psyche has suffered in this seemingly limited life, you remain every bit as brilliant and beautiful and limitless a spirit as your young self knew you were. Creator and the angels see your endless beauty and perfection. In this moment, invite the angels to wrap wings of love around you and help you remember you are a perfect being of love and light.

Wednesday: Archangel Gabriel

Wonders of the universe unfurl before you when you align with the light of your spirit. You are a keeper of Creator's song. Your soul holds the gift of creation. Consider that every thought and word are acts of creation. What transformation in grace might you set in motion today? Miracles begin with a single intention. Remember your spirit in each moment.

Thursday: Archangel Raphael

As you stand in the light, you provide a beacon for those who seek to heal. Release attachment to the pain and suffering that others may experience, for in order to assist them, you must maintain clarity within yourself. As an empath, you have the opportunity to perceive the feelings of those around you, but you need not carry their burdens. Rather, live as an example of how to rise beyond the turbulence.

Friday: Archangel Uriel

Each soul is held within the divine embrace. Have you ever wished to reciprocate that embrace, to give the Creator a hug? You can choose to return that gift by opening to the flow of love and allowing that perfect light to wash to and through you without qualification. Every time you pass on the love, offer the hope, expand the peace that is given to you, you repay that divine embrace. Like you, all of your fellow travelers are a part of God, and all kindnesses paid to them serve as a gift to the Creator. Will you extend love today? What ripples in the great sea of life may unfold when you do!

Saturday: Archangel Zadkiel

You may have wondered "what if" many times in your life, anchoring worry or challenges that might never come to pass. What if you anchored the potential for peace and joy, for benevolence and grace, for wonder and miracles instead? When your mind conjures worst-case scenarios, you have a choice to dwell on them and hold them in your body or to relinquish them to the Creator, forgive such notions, and quiet the worrying brain. What if the template for a more peaceful, blessed reality already over lit your being and your world this very instant? What if you were a vital part of bringing that reality into the fullness of being here on the Earth? Let that divine "what if" reside in your being, thus fueling the desires of your heart and soul.

Week 11

Sunday: Archangel Michael

Vigilantly armor yourself in the divine gifts of protection and discernment, and choose to ingest, digest, and live that which brings you into deeper kinship with the Light and greater alignment with your purpose. That which fills your life also colors your world. In every moment, you and the Creator are one. Thus, in every moment, you reveal to the Creator what you seek. Feel love and joy, and the Divine nourishes you with more of the same. That is your deepest calling now.

Monday: Archangel Jophiel

Joy in its finest essence expresses a soft, sweet wonderment. There is a peaceful quality to this kind of elation. Imagine floating up into the sky beyond all cares, being carried by the clouds on a sea of tranquil air while gentle sunbeams infuse you. This is one depiction of such joy. When you rise into the divine expression of joy, you experience the truth of infinite possibility and flowing creation. May your beloved heart know such joy here on Earth.

Tuesday: Archangel Chamuel

Every life you encounter—human, animal, plant, mineral—has consciousness and spirit. All are a part of the beautiful, blesséd creation known as planet Earth. Treat them tenderly. Offer compassion whenever possible. Recognize your kinship will all creatures. Bless each soul you pass along the highway of life.

Wednesday: Archangel Gabriel

It is time to build the foundation for your future. In deep contemplation, call on the Creator to awaken the vision of your most blessed life. Hold this dream within your heart and mind. Plant its seeds of light and let them take root as you nurture growth both from the Heavens and the Earth.

Thursday: Archangel Raphael

Are you acting as a steward of this wondrous world? Each soul is asked to live as a caretaker of the garden of Earth, to walk gently upon these shores for the span of a lifetime, and offer grace, gentleness, care, and kindness to all of God's creatures. Seek peace and harmony within and expand it to all life. Bring healing from the heart to this beautiful planet and honor this gracious gift of the Creator.

Friday: Archangel Uriel

Look at each circumstance, each emotion, each physical expression of your energetic needs as a guide and a teacher. In so doing, you allow yourself to move more quickly through these states on your way to becoming the highest version of yourself. Physical and emotional shifts are merely a part of the process. Embrace each lesson and continue to rise.

Saturday: Archangel Zadkiel

In the world around you, you see many results of limited and limiting mindsets. The word "impossible" opposes divine truth, for nothing lies outside potentiality in the infinite reality of the Creator of all. Which world will you choose to live in today? The angels abide ceaselessly in the eternal moment of benevolent creation, which is ever potent and powerful. The instant you decide to shift to a mindset of miracles, you join the angelic choirs in the realm of truth. No matter what you view in the outer world, you are invited to remain attuned to the higher reality you seek.

Week 12

Sunday: Archangel Michael

Blessings you have yet to imagine will manifest within your life when you align with divine will. Through meditation and prayer, open to the divine vision for your life. Surrender to the pull you feel toward your calling.

Monday: Archangel Jophiel

Inspiration flows forever from the Divine Heart through all life. Any of the travelers who cross your path can ignite the creative spark. All creatures great and small have a gift for you. All life has a blessing to share. When you are awake to the mystical and miraculous around you, you begin to hear the song of the wind, to see the shapes in the clouds, to discern the messengers in their many forms. Put on your magic glasses made of light. View the world through the lens of higher consciousness, and all that you behold will inspire your inner knowing and spirit's truth.

Tuesday: Archangel Chamuel

Do you recall that angel child you once were before the world limited your dreams? Today, if only for a moment, bring to life that memory and imagine living that dream. Let your flame of love nurture that child's aspiration. Embrace the wonder of your imagination with your caring heart.

Wednesday: Archangel Gabriel

Your view of yourself is likely profoundly different from the divine perception of your being. You were birthed in the Heart and Mind of Creator as a perfect, beautiful being of love, light, and creation. This truth lives throughout God Reality. The angels never identify you with the illusive human foibles and frailties on which you focus. Angelic beings only see the flawless, glorious truth of your spirit, untouched by the world in which you live. That vision is held for you by all who serve the Light. Imagine, if you will, a mirror of eternal truth where you may perceive yourself as the Creator does. And behold all that you can be.

Thursday: Archangel Raphael

Each day carries a signature of light that corresponds to a color. When you attune to that hue, you step into harmony with the rhythm of the universe. Ask the Divine each morning what color flows from Creation's Heart and allow the knowing of the answer to flow into your mind. You may be surprised at how many times this color shows up in the world around you—on the clothes of colleagues, in the flora you pass, and elsewhere in your surroundings. Let whatever shade of light adorns your world imprint upon your consciousness and saturate your feelings with its gifts, for each frequency in the rainbow shines with the perfect presence of the eternal.

Friday: Archangel Uriel

Are you aware of your inner gold? Within your sacred heart and ceaseless spirit, the same light flourishes that exists in the Heart and Mind of the Creator. Imagine the grace-filled golden and transcendent purple flames of peace expanding within you to form an alchemical reaction that burns through the baser aspects of human existence to illuminate the truer essence of wondrous light. Yes, child of light, you are golden. Remember this truth of your spirit.

Saturday: Archangel Zadkiel

All exists within the great oneness, and all live in kinship with one another, yet each soul is also unique. Creator makes no duplicates. Celebrate both your similarities and your distinctiveness. Each note in the great symphony of the universe is vital to the composition. The violin and the cello sing sweetly together. The tenor, the baritone, and the bass harmonize into glorious perfection. Recognize that you are both the singer, the song, the instrument, and an essential part of the infinite opus. Give thanks for your unique, glorious song and walk in harmony with the other melodies that join together in the beautiful refrain known as Earth.

Week 13

Sunday: Archangel Michael

Are you the one to whom others turn when they seek a safe place to land amid the troubles of the world? If so, you are a protector spirit, a guardian, who seeks to watch over loved ones. You have far more strength than you know. Angels of the Light abide with you. Trust that you and those you love are held in divine embrace.

Monday: Archangel Jophiel

What if every moment of joy you have ever felt reverberated forever through the eternal realms? What if each creation born of your own pure heart lived on forever in the Mind and Heart of God? And the Creator holds them all in high regard—from that little boy's fingerpainting to that master artist's finest piece. Every composition, every song, every note and chord of creation remains an everlasting testament to your life. What joy might you bring today to the whole of the universe? What wonder may you create?

Tuesday: Archangel Chamuel

Locate a photograph of yourself as a child. Gaze deeply and intently upon that youthful face that you once wore. What do you discern there—innocence, playfulness, joy, or something else? Perhaps wounds had already etched upon the heart of that little one. This child is important. This child needs your love today. Since time is merely a construct, you can easily send compassion, love, hope, and reassurance to the youth you were. Expand love from your heart until it fills your being, call on the Light of Spirit, and send through the passages of time every word of cherishing, every kind intention, and all the love you hold in your powerful spirit to heal, soothe, and bless that child. Doing so may change your life.

Wednesday: Archangel Gabriel

The veil between this world and the next is not made of stone. It is merely a glimmer of light. Those you love who have traveled beyond these shores still hear your calls. Love is the eternal song carried between this life and the next. It is the garment of each soul who transcends the physical and rises to the heavenly realms. Send them your love, and they will receive that blessing.

Thursday: Archangel Raphael

Do you perceive the world around you as a sacred place? Is your home merely a habitat where you pass your days and nights, or do you view it as a space where miracles may occur and dreams may begin to flourish and take shape? Is your workplace a building filled with people and furnishings, or is it a place to find kinship, to bridge divides, to build relationships, and bring blessings to pass? Is the forest or park or seaside where you spend your spare hours a setting of wonder where marvels abound, a sanctuary for the senses, or just another thicket or trail or beach? Your perception of the world determines your reality. Are you willing to see the sacred in all life and in your surroundings today?

Friday: Archangel Uriel

Deep within the sea, where the slow-moving currents flow, the song of the ocean still may be heard, but the turbulence and storms, the crashing waves of the world near the surface remain distant. Whatever tumult arises in your world today, remember the deeper currents within you where calmer waters reside. Allow yourself to pull back from whatever unfolds and find the still point. Breathe in peace and remember your oneness with Creation's Heart.

Saturday: Archangel Zadkiel

Go to the place where you feel most at home. It may be a quiet chapel, a room in your abode, or another kind of sanctuary such as a peaceful glade or a lonely strand of beach. For some, your refuge may not be a place so much as a state of being, a quieting of the mind. Spend time in the space where you find solace. There, in the restorative surroundings of your choice, call Spirit close to you. Accept the power and essence of divine love that is ever present just beyond the periphery of waking life. Claim respite from the mundane world and align with the Light, which remains your truest home. When it is time to return to what most humans deem the "real world," remember and carry this pure rest with you.

Week 14

Sunday: Archangel Michael

Awaken more fully the splendid gifts of perception that came with your soul into this world. It is time to reach a new level of awareness, to align your energy to a higher frequency. Envision a brilliant blue light flowing from the Heart of Creation to clear the pathways of thought and emotion and reveal a greater resonance with the realms of light.

Monday: Archangel Jophiel

The butterfly with the injured wing still flits from flower to flower, drinking deeply of the sweet nectar of life until its final moment. All children of light who enter the world of form come to know the sting of pain, loss, and injury, yet you still may find the joys and beauty of life. Days of honeyed sweetness, treasured moments yet to be, live already in the Heart of Creation, waiting for you to take a step toward them or, better yet, to run headlong into the embrace of a finer future. Give thanks for every instant and ounce of happiness. Celebrate jubilantly each small victory on your path to greater joy. In so doing, you send the message, "Beloved Creator, I am ready."

Tuesday: Archangel Chamuel

At the end of your day or at any time you need a break from the energies swirling around you, imagine yourself standing beneath a waterfall made of liquid light. Its waters contain a myriad of soft pastel colors that wash over, around, and even through you. Let this vision expand throughout your being as you call upon the heart light of Creator to cleanse from the mind, body, and energy field all that is out of harmony with your true nature of love, grace, peace, and joy.

Wednesday: Archangel Gabriel

All of life has a song. Each star, planet, plant, mineral, animal, and human exudes a harmonic that is heard always by the angels and by Spirit. This great chorus resounds throughout the universe, yet the Creator knows and hears each single note, each soul, each life among the infinite multitude. In the deepest silence of your sacred heart, you may hear a quiet hum or a soft tune played as if far in the distance. The song of your soul calls to you. Listen today for its gentle calling and remember who you are.

Thursday: Archangel Raphael

How do you measure the days of your life? For an angel, the answer is simple. Begin each day with the question, "How may I be of service today?" When all that transpires serves the highest good, each day is a testament to blessings both offered and received.

Friday: Archangel Uriel

A stone tossed into calm waters sends ripples in all directions. Similarly, you extend your light into the world wherever you pass. Each kind deed, each expression of joy and love, and each moment of peace reverberate into the world. When you are emitting the light of your spirit, people may smile more when you are around. Those who are brave enough to speak up may mention that your presence makes them feel lighter or more uplifted. Will you join with the angels and radiate peace today?

Saturday: Archangel Zadkiel

Self-recrimination cannot pave the way to peace. It merely anchors in your mind, body, and being the issue for which you blame yourself. Seek instead forgiveness of self and of all that is out of harmony with your spirit's truth. Dive into a violet pool of divine forgiveness and bathe in the waters of mercy. Whatever actions, thoughts, or words created imbalance and disharmony, these may be cleansed in the divine heart light. Then, rise beyond the issue that prompted feelings of self-blame. Make the decision to let go of the programming behind that action or those words. Evolve and create a new pattern. Each time you act on that new pattern, you strengthen it.

Week 15

Sunday: Archangel Michael

On this day and throughout this week, focus on conscious expression. Your words reflect your inner being and have the power to create. Pause in every interaction before responding. Let kindness color your viewpoint. Construct your conversations with care. The more you practice speaking with honor, the more you give voice to the Light.

Monday: Archangel Jophiel

The mind can take you on many journeys, some glorious and others less jubilant. The higher mind, the wisdom of Spirit, has only one destination: blessings. Imagine that you can link your human conscious mind to the pure light of your spirit. As you conceive of such a wonder, you build a bridge easily traversed. Let your mind wander upward into the over-lighting consciousness of your spirit, which resides forever in the infinite Mind of God. Take a few moments each day to perceive that pathway and connect to the universal and eternal. In so doing, you begin to walk consciously through the world and to lift your perceptions to a more beneficent, loving state.

Tuesday: Archangel Chamuel

The way to peace lies through the gate of love. Without love's soothing presence and perfect essence, the path to inner peace remains blocked. Can you remember a time when you felt love profoundly, unconditionally? The memory of such a moment can serve as your guiding star. Focus on that memory. Let go of any subsequent grief or longing. Just move into the moment when you felt that kind of love and expand that feeling through your heart, mind, body, being. Revel in it. And recognize the sense of overwhelming peace that resides in this pure love. Carry this love with you into the world.

Wednesday: Archangel Gabriel

Every soul who walks the Earth encounters periods of strife or challenge and moments when hope falters. The angels invite you to rekindle your most cherished hopes and form them into the hallowed words of the heart. Speak them to Spirit with a love so powerful that no illusion or shadow can block the truth of your intentions. Joyfully accept your prayer as the reality that over lights your being now and builds the dream you hold dear. Today, sound the horn of hope to light the path for self and for all who seek enlightenment.

Thursday: Archangel Raphael

A higher knowledge than may be accessed in any earthly tome lives in the light of every soul and anchors in the pure, sacred heart within you. Creator's essence lives in your spirit. Communing with Spirit, however this unfolds for you, provides an endless source of understanding and grace. Seek the sacred heart within and the wisdom of Spirit. Therein lives the eternal.

Friday: Archangel Uriel

How intertwined the path of charity and the road to peace! Every kindness you share in this world brings you one step closer to serenity. Compassion is a divine quality that reveals spirit in action and leads to transcendence. Let your heart guide your hands, your words, your being. Your benevolence ushers peace into this world and clears the path for lasting accord.

Saturday: Archangel Zadkiel

The exquisite lotus whose blossoms express serene beauty grows only in mud. Experiencing the fullness of beauty requires facing life's challenges and growing into your wisdom. As you confront life's obstacles, call upon the Creator to cleanse those blocks and to free you from that which has chained you to old patterns and issues. In doing so, you may begin to view the world from a more divine perspective.

Week 16

Sunday: Archangel Michael

Now is not the time to give up or lose hope. Despite setbacks and challenges on your path, look to the Divine with a hopeful, trusting heart. Faith is the shield that clothes you in divine power. Seek deep within your heart the light of faith that will enable you to move forward.

Monday: Archangel Jophiel

Rewriting the patterns of the mind through the grace of the Spirit requires focus upon the Light. Let every breath be one of light and love. Empower yourself each day by embracing only that which you deem aligned with the Divine. Discern your emotions and let them teach you what is in harmony with your journey to wholeness and wisdom.

Tuesday: Archangel Chamuel

A continuous stream of love and life force expands throughout the universe. This light cannot be denied to any soul except by one's own choice. In each situation, ask yourself if you are blocking or opening to love. Anger, unforgiveness, and all forms of fear impede the flow of blessings. Invite Creator's purest Love to blaze through all obstructions.

Wednesday: Archangel Gabriel

Clarify the channels of thought, emotion, and energy in order to rise into divine creation. The power to shift your reality flows through light. Wash old mental patterns, programs, and constructs that keep you mired in the past and limit both your awareness and your focus/clear thinking. As you relinquish mental congestion of dissonant energies and replace these with hopeful, harmonious thought patterns, you alter the world around you.

Thursday: Archangel Raphael

Profound healing is a sacred dance between the heart, mind, body, spirit, and Creator. Expand the light of the heart to encompass your mind, body, and complete being. Call on the healing angels and the grace and healing power of the Creator. Along with the curatives of this world, open a space for miracles and follow the path to wholeness that lies within.

Friday: Archangel Uriel

Your mind is capable of creating countless scenarios that bring unrest. Remember that the turmoil of the ego is mere illusion. You have the power and grace to choose a different path. Your spirit holds only peace. When the mind turns toward the shadow, rest within Spirit's embrace. Call on the silence. Anchor the peace.

Saturday: Archangel Zadkiel

Transmutation alters the nature or quality of any substance. Through deep forgiveness, all past pains and offenses lose their power. Walk into the sacred spiritual fires that hold no heat. Imagine and intend that all that is less than blessed transmute into love.

Week 17

Sunday: Archangel Michael

Faith untested lacks substance. When you can hold faith amid chaos and fear, you have risen to the next level of understanding and truth. Faith can conquer fear and disturbance only when it is fully secured to the psyche. Call on the Divine to imprint the pure essence of faith in your mind. Hold faith through the storms of life, and you will rise beyond the need for it into the knowing that all is in divine order.

Monday: Archangel Jophiel

Each life is a tale of wonder. The outline of the story comes to life before your first breath as a newborn, but the finer details are written by you. Together with Creator, you weave the tapestry of time. Into each circumstance, you inscribe the meaningful moments and glean the wisdom that propels you further into the tale. What shall your story say today, this week, this month, this year? Will you join in conscious co-creation and drive the plot forward towards the beautiful truth of your spirit?

Tuesday: Archangel Chamuel

Honor the wisdom of your heart. Along with your spirit, that vessel of love serves as your truest guide on the path of life. When mental energy becomes overwhelming, sink into the heart space and connect to the deeper truth that all are one within the great Light of Creation. That infinite essence always holds you, but sometimes in the turbulent waters of this world, you need to remind yourself what is real. Your heart always knows.

Wednesday: Archangel Gabriel

A silent communication happens every moment of the day. Everything in the universe is made of energy, and energy interacts constantly. Your emotions and thoughts exude frequencies as do those of the people you encounter and of all life around you. In addition, divine energies flow ceaselessly into all aspects of life. Become aware of this endless exchange. Pay attention to the circulation of energy. Doing so will allow you to avoid situations that don't align with your light and will guide you to higher frequency experiences.

Thursday: Archangel Raphael

Your environment can contribute significantly to the ease you experience in your daily life. True comfort can never be found in chaos. When you do something each day to contribute to the flow of your space, soon your entire life begins to feel different. Serene, soothing bedrooms offer a greater chance for deep sleep. Uncluttered kitchens allow greater sustenance to flow into your life. Small changes can shift your world.

Friday: Archangel Uriel

To what do you offer your devotion? Are you dedicating your energy, time, thought, imagination, feeling to that which is temporal or to that which is eternal? Your heart knows the answer to this question. It is never too late to transcend the mundane reality and live aligned with the Light. Simply turn your awareness, your focus, your presence toward the wonders of Creation to begin to embody and live the miracles forever available within the infinite.

Saturday: Archangel Zadkiel

No matter what disturbance occurs in your life, the divine essence remains changeless. At the end of each day and each week, set aside a time to shed the stresses and release the cares you have encountered. Imagine a great bonfire into which you may toss those troubles and envision them being consumed by the sacred flames of transmutation. You were never meant to carry the burdens of the world nor to allow worry to inhabit your consciousness. Open the space for finer feelings and joyful experiences by letting go.

Week 18

Sunday: Archangel Michael

Neither the voice of ego nor the noise of the multitude can change the course of the heart and the spirit. The deepest part of you knows more fully and profoundly what is real. Remember that the Divine is ever loving, kind, and peaceful. The shadow within and without may seek to imitate these traits, but only the Light holds itself in love. Seek then your inner knowing in the heart's essence of love and light. There you will find the wisdom you require and know the wonder of love.

Monday: Archangel Jophiel

Let go of the autopilot mindset that permits stagnation. Live, breathe, speak, think, act with intention. Set an intention in gratitude as you rise each morning. Remember to observe your thoughts, words, and actions throughout the day to discern how well you are aligning with that intention. Shift your mindset into greater love and light each time you catch yourself steering away from your intended course.

Tuesday: Archangel Chamuel

Love heals. Love reveals. Love builds. Love fulfills. Love lives. Love forgives. Love sustains. Love remains. Love is the ultimate goal of every single soul. When all else is gone, love is the spirit's song. Let the love of your precious heart shine into the world today.

Wednesday: Archangel Gabriel

On what have you built the foundation of your life? Temporal sands shift with the seasons, but your spirit remains true and unaltered. When your footing rests upon the solid ground of the eternal, your path remains certain no matter the obstacles you perceive. Deepen your connection to Spirit and let love guide your footsteps.

Thursday: Archangel Raphael

Family means more than the circle of your birth. Gather to you those whose light lives in kinship with your own, those fellow travelers with whom your affinity runs deep. You recognize and trust one another instantly. Your lights shine a little more brightly in each other's presence. You feel more truly yourself when they are near. You bolster one another. Welcome and give thanks for such blessings in your life.

Friday: Archangel Uriel

Listen with your heart today. Even passing conversations take on deeper meaning when the heart is open to genuine understanding. Profound listening is a vital part of supporting those around you and essential to true communication and to the cause of peace. You may become a valued confidante, a cherished friend or partner, and an indispensable coworker by offering this gift.

Saturday: Archangel Zadkiel

Kindle a sense of conscience. The heart already holds highest integrity in infinite measure, so let the human consciousness learn this vital gift to avoid injuring others. A strong conscience guides the mind to honor and lovingly regard those who share the journey. Conscience breeds gentleness, respect, and benevolent interaction.

Week 19

Sunday: Archangel Michael

The angels abide with you in your service here on Earth. You are never alone. What dreams may come to fruition when you accept your path fully?! Access your divine purpose within your heart and spirit.

Monday: Archangel Jophiel

Joy will find the heart that is open to it. No matter how much there is to grieve, this world also holds the potential for untold blessings. Look for the little miracles—the wildflower bursting forth through concrete, the bird nesting on a tiny windowsill, that unexpected gust of cooling breeze on a hot day, the butterfly flitting by at just the right moment to catch your eye, the smiles of children, the sound of laughter, all the tiny marvels that may have escaped your notice if not for the ageless innocent within you who remembers that treasures may be found around the next corner. If you've gotten lost in life's sorrows or worries, invite that inner child to help you find the precious joys along your path.

Tuesday: Archangel Chamuel

Child of light, you are precious beyond your capacity to perceive. Open your heart to receive the love and blessings that flow forever from the Divine Heart. Then, be that blessing for all you touch.

Wednesday: Archangel Gabriel

Deep in the Heart of Light lies the story of your soul. Know that you came to this world to do nothing less than express your eternal light. Realize the dream. Awaken to the glory. Become the sweet essence of your unique spirit, for you are gifted in ways you have yet to perceive.

Thursday: Archangel Raphael

Sharing and caring are two cornerstones of divine relationship. Share the truths and wisdom of your heart and genuinely cherish your companions in life. Your relationships will flourish when you cultivate a two-way flow of these gifts. A single soul has the power to open the current of kindness and unlock the heart to the same in return.

Friday: Archangel Uriel

The gift of each day awaits your exploration. The dawn whispers, "What glory shall we experience? What wonders may we create?" The sunrise always carries its pure potential as the sky breathes light into the waking world. Unwrap the present that awaits with a grateful heart and let the blessings find you.

Saturday: Archangel Zadkiel

When the angels see you dreaming of a better world and holding that vision inside your heart, they send light to that desire. They join with you to fan the flames of the heart and create a brighter future. Will you join with the angels to expand your love and nourish that vision until all life lifts into your dream? Remember, worry will only limit that divine reality you seek, while belief and love will nurture it.

Week 20

Sunday: Archangel Michael

The dissonance you see in the world arises from the clash between the old shadow reality and the waves of light and love that shift life into a more peaceful existence. The Divine is spurring every soul to relinquish the path of fear and lift into the gift of harmony. Pay attention to the emotional tides within and around you. Are you giving power to separation and fear, thereby contributing to the great divide, or are you maintaining kindness, grace, and love in the face of division and discord? You have the power to choose—always.

Monday: Archangel Jophiel

The solar heart of inspiration shines upon all willing souls. When you feel stuck or life seems stagnant, you may tap into the creative pulse of the universe. Envision the golden-white solar light beaming directly into your mind, heart, body, and soul. Imagine and intend that you become an extension of that light in this world, radiating its rays from your core. Thus, creation's light may illuminate your life.

Tuesday: Archangel Chamuel

How many times have you felt that no one understood you, that you were lost and alone in an uncaring world? In such moments, it is difficult for the human mind to comprehend the ceaseless connection to the eternal. Rest assured that someone always embraces you. Someone constantly prays for you. Someone always hopes for your highest outcomes and believes in you. Your guardian angel forever cherishes you and invisibly stands with you, treasuring your soul, even in this moment.

Wednesday: Archangel Gabriel

How can you prize the gemstones and creations of this world and fail to recognize the beauty of your own being? The rarest pearl formed in the purest waters cannot surpass the light of your wondrous spirit. Angels even now whisper into your heart and mind how deeply you are loved, how great a treasure you are to all within the unseen realms. Trust that you can make a difference today in ways you have yet to imagine. Begin by recognizing the divine within yourself. All else flows from that.

Thursday: Archangel Raphael

Divine consciousness stretches to infinity and into eternity. Your truest self, your spirit, lives in oneness with that Light. Allow this concept to permeate your senses. Let it sink from your soul into your mind. With every breath you take today, speak your oneness with the infinite into yourself. In that knowing, open to boundless blessings.

Friday: Archangel Uriel

The sun is always rising somewhere. That quiet yet potent moment of infinite potential is ever dawning. Breathe in its radiance, peace, and glorious light, and let your psyche bathe in wonder. Live in the knowing that all things are possible.

Saturday: Archangel Zadkiel

Child of light, you pave the path to peace when you can forgive yourself as well as others. Recognize that every seeming fault and flaw may be shifted into grace. See each day as a new opportunity to rise and transform. Identify what within your life needs to change, deeply forgive, and cleanse all past examples of this issue. Then, begin to alter the mindset, the patterns, and the actions through gentle but determined measures.

Week 21

Sunday: Archangel Michael

Every emotion and thought carries a vibrational frequency and wave. Your feelings affect those around you just as their energies affect you. Shelter yourself within divine embrace as you move through the world so the waves of discord remain separate from your psyche. As much as possible, choose today to align with and emit the energy of love, peace, and grace.

Monday: Archangel Jophiel

Don't miss the miracles along your path. Coincidence and chance are only words for divine hands at work. Listen to your inner voice. Follow the signs so often sent to you. Wonders abound all around you when you truly look.

Tuesday: Archangel Chamuel

The Divine sees you trying. Every time you make the effort to rise beyond the challenges you face, to lift your heart and eyes to the Light, to look beyond the shadow and see the essence of Spirit in all, to offer a helping hand to those in need, the angels celebrate. You are making a difference—even when you cannot discern that truth. You are contributing love to the greater whole. You are changing the world for the better. So keep moving steadily toward where you want to be. And if you falter, the angels will lift you back onto the path.

Wednesday: Archangel Gabriel

Creation is eternal. Can you hear its ceaseless song? The great composer invites you to stop sitting on the periphery of life. Will you consciously join the dance? Set your intentions. Breathe life into them. Ignite the fires within and expand your dreams into the world. You already know the steps to the sacred dance. They exist in your spirit, and the rhythm of your song anchors in every heartbeat. Listen. The music plays for you.

Thursday: Archangel Raphael

Healing unfolds as the heart is ready. Every wound builds a wall unless you work diligently to forgive and release. Seek, then, to dissolve the barriers within, to relinquish the pains held in body and mind, to let go of the impediments to the perfect flow of love and grace. The body remembers each injury until it is freed of that hurt. Wash in the waters of life and healing. Let all that once was seep into the eternal wellspring where it becomes as clear and pure as the infinite sea of Spirit.

Friday: Archangel Uriel

You are here to love and learn, to progress and to discern. The great classroom known as Earth offers abundant opportunities for spiritual evolution. You have the potential to grow into your true self, to live vibrantly and consciously, if you rise to the occasion of truly living. So many possible pathways exist in a single day. Consider this. As you align with higher awareness, the optimal paths will become apparent. Many signposts present themselves along the way. Look for them and you will find them. Connect to your heart and soul and the most ideal route becomes clear.

Saturday: Archangel Zadkiel

The bridge to forever lies through the truth of the spirit. You walk between the worlds of past and future, but the way forward lives in the now. Seek the truest path within the eternal moment. The more present you are, the easier it is to attune to the light of the soul, to remain aware of the energies around you, to align with blessings you would otherwise miss. Attend to this moment and the next will unfold divinely.

Week 22

Sunday: Archangel Michael

Trusting the Divine requires a leap of faith. Leaving control of all potential outcomes in divine hands requires a profound sense of surrender. Prayer without faith is empty and meaningless. When you live and breathe faith, honoring the highest potential for blessings, you give to God your desire and allow the Creator to bring to pass that which is most aligned.

Monday: Archangel Jophiel

What fears do you harbor in the recesses of your mind? No matter how hidden they may be from others or from yourself, their presence reflects in your life. When something seems amiss in the outer world, the wise soul always asks what within needs to shift. The more fully you can clear those cobwebs of consciousness, the doubts and worries, the more quickly your life may reveal beneficial changes.

Tuesday: Archangel Chamuel

Wherever you travel, as you move through the world you leave traces of your light behind. Whatever you touch with love and tenderness holds that gift as an imprint forever. Your precious essence lingers upon all life long after you leave the physical realm. But more than this. Every moment of grace you have ever shared is written into the eternal song of your life and into Creator's infinite heart and mind. So it is with all those who have passed through the veil.

Wednesday: Archangel Gabriel

The human psyche requires relief from the fray. You discover your greatest ease and grace when you rise into your spirit. As you lie snugly in your bed or sit quietly in a restful place, imagine that you can dance upon the wind. Join with your spirit and lift beyond the clouds, far above the crowds, to a space of peace. You may find the finest respite in the soul's embrace. When you return your consciousness to the seemingly solid world, ground this sense of serenity and rest within your being.

Thursday: Archangel Raphael

You likely have experienced physical cravings and emotional yearnings in your life, but have you experienced spiritual thirst? The deepest desires stem from the soul, and no amount of earthly fulfillment can quench such longing. Only genuine connection to the spirit, to Creator, to eternal, infinite Love can satisfy such desire. Seek, then, to embrace the light of your spirit and fully express it in the world of form, to live the unique perfection of Creation's Light that your soul was born to communicate. The finest cuisine cannot sate the soul's need for communion with the Creator. But prayer and meditation in the Light can saturate the consciousness with grace untold.

Friday: Archangel Uriel

In your soul, a fire burns, a passion for the path you came to walk. You may not have discovered it. You may even seem to have meandered through life never quite settling upon a meaningful calling. Nonetheless, your spirit remembers the higher purpose that expresses through your being even when you remain unaware on the earthly level of existence. Every step guides you to that mission no matter how far afield it may seem in the moment.

Saturday Archangel Zadkiel

Set aside some time to walk in the natural world. Breathe the sky into your heart. Let the sun shine upon your soul. Transform into the tranquil truth of your spirit. Imagine that every sunbeam showers you with cleansing light. Every raindrop washes you in divine peace. The light of transcendence abounds in nature and restores your mind to greater calm and your heart to joy and wonder.

Week 23

Sunday: Archangel Michael

It is time to move beyond the mire and the struggles. Surrender to God's wisdom and grace. When greeted by challenges and difficulties, ask within yourself, "How am I blocking the flow of love?" Yielding to the Divine is the only true course. Imbalance reveals itself through pain. Find balance in the divine direction of your spirit. This is the pathway to peace and wholeness.

Monday: Archangel Jophiel

There is a light in you that no one and nothing can extinguish. What the Creator brings into being is forever unalterable. The tides of life may cause many shifts in your world and in your human consciousness, but the real self remains as pure and perfect as the moment your spirit was born. Tap into that inner truth, and breathe, live, love, and honor the eternal light you are.

Tuesday: Archangel Chamuel

Rather than measuring your day by minutes and hours, consider the number of kindnesses you can show, the amount of love you can expand into the world. How many smiles, kind words, cordial greetings, and loving gestures can you offer today? Fill your heart with love as you begin your day and see where it takes you.

Wednesday: Archangel Gabriel

Open your mind to the true strength held within your heart. A seedling of thought nourished with profound love can grow your divine dreams and build bridges to the wonders and joys you seek to embrace and embody.

Thursday: Archangel Raphael

Abundant blessings flow to those with open hearts and minds. The more your psyche focuses on the beauty and blessings of life and your heart emits loving, joyful resonances, the more easily you attune to miracles and clear the path to wonders.

Friday: Archangel Uriel

May your psyche be soothed in the peace that flows from Creator's heart. May your consciousness rise in joy as divine light enfolds you. May you know in each moment that you are infinitely loved.

Saturday: Archangel Zadkiel

Challenging times present every soul with a choice. When the world screams in anguish or the multitude utters madness, will you give in to circumstance and dive into self-pity or become a voice of kindness, a beacon of love, a light shining in the darkness? Whatever upheaval exists in the world outside your door or even within your own thoughts, you have the power to move out of reaction into the quiet song of the heart and find solace, sustenance, and respite.

Week 24

Sunday: Archangel Michael

Fulfillment comes when you align with your soul's truth. Have you not heard the small voice within you calling in your quiet moments? You know what you are meant to do. Your heart of light answers every question. Listen and live the truth of your inner knowing.

Monday: Archangel Jophiel

You and the stars themselves are one, for each is of that same matter born of Creator's Mind and Heart. Seek the starlight essence of your spirit, the very truth of your being. It shines forever within your core and encompasses all that you are. Trust your luminous soul, which ever guides you. And know with certainty that you are a wonder, a marvel of creation, a perfect child of light. Accept this and rise into a higher reality.

Tuesday: Archangel Chamuel

The pot of gold at the end of the rainbow lives in your own heart. The unending wellspring of creative essence flows through your life stream. As you inspire others to awaken to the wisdom of their own hearts, the divine ignites within you the gifts of your spirit.

Wednesday: Archangel Gabriel

A constant exchange exists between you and the Divine. Energies move endlessly into and through all aspects of creation. Divine inspiration remains ever at hand in the great outpouring from the Eternal Mind and Heart. An answer exists for every problem you face. An alternative path awaits when any door closes. Guidance comes from moment to moment for those able to and willing to listen with the openness of a child. Imagine turning a radio dial and coming upon an infinite number of stations, all offering a unique frequency to assist you at any moment. This is how the angels view life. Only the mindset, the thoughts, blocks, and patterns you have established and repeated impede these transmissions. Your work then is to unblock, to dissolve, to release those impediments and mental constructs that clutter the senses. In so doing, all that can benefit your cause floods your being.

Thursday: Archangel Raphael

Let your home become a haven for your heart. From the colors in each room to the treasured mementos of your life, fill your space with reminders of who you truly are. Allow your inner being to reflect into your outer world as much as you can. In this way, you cultivate caring, harmonious energies and a healing atmosphere.

Friday: Archangel Uriel

In the potent pause between breaths lives a moment of perfection—outside of time, immersed in the ethers. Lean into that pause, the reflective instant, and find your center. Feel the gratitude at your core for the blessings yet to come. Believe and bathe in that reality. Live that truth. As you do, you begin to walk into a brighter future.

Saturday: Archangel Zadkiel

Listen, look, feel, and sense. The Divine whispers messages into your heart each day. All that crosses your path has wisdom to impart. Today, watch for the signals from Spirit. Even your memories may have a message. Learn to translate the communication that comes when your open heart moves through the world.

Week 25

Sunday: Archangel Michael

Your prayers, your seeking, will be answered with love. The Divine cherishes you. Every moment of your life has meaning, for you shine into the world what only you may offer. Be still and open the space for blessings. Know that Creator is with you.

Monday: Archangel Jophiel

Serenity lives in the simple joys of life. Recognize that every single second holds the potential for miracles. The more you perceive the miraculous in the mundane, the more you discover the gold of your true self. Surrender to the sacred moment by observing the beauty and wonder all around you.

Tuesday: Archangel Chamuel

Love is the greatest gift in existence. Its essence is pure and healing. Love abides at the core of every heart, and all souls have access to its blessings, yet the path to receive or to freely give it may be blocked by fear at times. You have the power to hold the open space for love to flow into every particle of your existence from the inner core, the sacred space within. Call on the Divine, your own spirit's pure light and the Creator of all, to flood your heart, mind, body, and being with that precious gift of divine love. In this way, the channel for love may flow in both directions, and its pure grace paves the path to blessings.

Wednesday: Archangel Gabriel

No matter how far you may fall, there is always an angel there to lift you. Your own angel guardians even now pray for your rising beyond whatever issues you face. This is true for each person who walks upon the Earth. As you peer through the mist of illusion and behold the beauty and grace of those who hold you ever in love and light, you begin to understand that you are never alone, and countless beings of light cheer you on in every moment.

Thursday: Archangel Raphael

To say thank you from the heart is to sing the light of the soul. Those words enriched with the emanation of love reach into the heart of the one who receives them and touch the pure essence of spirit. "Thank you" and "I love you" spoken with meaning and depth of feeling carry a charge of divine grace.

Friday: Archangel Uriel

You are much more than the trappings of your daily life. You are as radiant as the sun-kissed clouds at dawn and as beautiful as the silken azure sky. You, precious soul, are a wonder of divine creation, and only you can live your light each day. Right now, just in this moment, remember and breathe the truth of your spirit.

Saturday: Archangel Zadkiel

Your truest self holds the vision of your eternal nature, your perfect essence. As you shift and transform, embrace hope and love, those gifts of the heart, and align always with your divine dream and your spirit's light. You welcome miracle moments when you do so.

Week 26

Sunday: Archangel Michael

The shadows have striven to mute your voice, to dim your light, yet you remain steadfast in your intentions. Continue to cleanse and heal. Remember that the resonance of fear is no match for the Love you anchor within your spirit. Illuminate your inner being with greater levels of light. Nothing can stop your progress except you.

Monday: Archangel Jophiel

May winged joy lift your spirits. May you imbibe wonder and delight. Like the blossoms coming to life in springtime, may you feel the renewal of the eternal wellspring from which all blessings flow. You are co-creating every moment, so why not look for the joy today and discover it was yours all along?

Tuesday: Archangel Chamuel

Genuine friends walk with you through the valleys and climb beside you to the mountaintop. When your steps falter, they hold a hand to steady you. And when you soar, they celebrate. Your angel guardians, your constant companions in this life, serve in profound friendship all your days. Remember they walk by your side even now and invite you to honor the path you came to walk and extend love to all life as they do in each moment of existence.

Wednesday: Archangel Gabriel

From the heights, angels descend to utter gentle guidance. Their voices speak more softly than the wind and can be heard only in the silence. Seek the quiet within and connect to the eternal essence of the Sacred Heart. Listen with the purest intentions. You will hear what is needed when you calm the senses and open to the peace that flows from the angelic realm.

Thursday: Archangel Raphael

The greatest blessing of this life lies in finding your way home to the heart and living the light of the spirit. From moment to moment, you choose the path to draw closer to that loving essence or push aside the pure grace of the heart and soul. Check in with your inner aspect as often as possible throughout the day. Hold and expand gratitude. In mere moments, you can return to center and realign to your truer self.

Friday: Archangel Uriel

A haven lives within your heart and soul, a place where you remain untouched by the turmoil and troubles of the outer world. At times, when you feel buffeted by the storms of life, you seek that refuge and seem unable to reach Spirit's safe harbor. The tempest cannot affect you when you anchor daily in that light of peace. Cultivate the sanctuary of your spirit every day. Become so secured in its serene waters that whatever storm rages in your life, you remain moored and sheltered.

Saturday: Archangel Zadkiel

Spirit is changeless yet ever evolving. The human psyche seemingly shifts with the tides, but the soul resides in constant resonance with the infinite and everlasting. As you move through the world today, be mindful of the immutable nature of your true self. See each experience as a means to move into greater harmony with your spirit. Look to the eternal for the knowing that allows you to align in each moment with the person you truly are.

Week 27

Sunday: Archangel Michael

You have more courage and strength than you realize. Relinquish the fear of living your power, for you have the balance and wisdom to temper such strength with love and grace. Once you allow the Light to flow freely through you, shining fully without resistance, you will attract all you seek and become an even greater blessing to those you love.

Monday: Archangel Jophiel

Do you believe more than you can see with human eyes—that laughter sparkles and happy tears glow, that wonder lies just around the next corner and in your own soul, that stardust and miracles live in your heart, that you and the universe are one, inseparable and eternal? The child of light you truly are believes in all these things and much more. Tune in to that wondrous innocence and believe, for only those who believe can truly see.

Tuesday: Archangel Chamuel

Such depth of love abides within your heart. In the realms of light, you existed as pure love. You are here on the Earth to learn to love unconditionally as a human. Share love with all you touch. Open fully to love within your own life; cherish your spirit and all souls as the Divine cherishes you.

Wednesday: Archangel Gabriel

In viewing only the visible spectrum, you cannot perceive the angelic realm, yet those unseen beings walk among you constantly. The legions of light are vast and remain ever present. When you lift your eyes unto the Light and raise your conscious awareness to a higher resonance, you may sense the invisible helpers who dedicate themselves to enhancing your life and your world. Even now, know that you are heard. Your prayers are held in the ethereal heart of every angel who guides, protects, and loves you.

Thursday: Archangel Raphael

So much of what passes for reality is mere illusion. Disturbance on the physical level, no matter how real it seems, exists outside the deeper truth. The eternal reality is one of beauty, grace, love, and peace. The true essence of your being never suffers nor does it know any challenge. Your spirit holds the keys to a more gracious life. As you align your consciousness more with your everlasting nature, you blossom into a more fully realized version of yourself and recognize that the vagaries of illusion can never hold sway upon your sacred self.

Friday: Archangel Uriel

Serenely speak into your mind these words of grace: "I am the infinite stream of divine love and light washing through me now. I am the infinite flow of peace to self and to all." Trust that as you affirm these higher truths a wave of light passes through you, clearing the pathways of thought and opening the meridians of tranquility.

Saturday: Archangel Zadkiel

To decree is to speak into being the desires of the heart and soul. Powerfully and lovingly affirm your intentions. Pray with meaning and heartfelt fervor. A prayer spoken with the love, power, and grace of the spirit sends a mighty signal to the universe.

Week 28

Sunday: Archangel Michael

Birthing your true self requires labor. You are prepared for the task. Remember that great blessings follow the labor pains. Be steadfast in your dedication to honoring your truth. Integrate the divine energies flowing to you. Child of light, your essence, your spirit calls you to grow into your path and welcome miracles.

Monday: Archangel Jophiel

What a wealth of wonder abounds in this world. Drink deeply of the sweet nectar of life. Savor every moment of this gift. No other experience in all of creation compares. Do not take a single breath for granted nor squander an instant of this miracle of human life. Recognize the richness of sensory existence and give thanks by basking in the glory of each moment.

Tuesday: Archangel Chamuel

Seek to love yourself as the Creator loves you—without condition or reservation and with the fullness of your sacred heart. Consider that level of love. Bring to mind the greatest love you have ever experienced and multiply it by infinity. That is Creator's love for you, the perfect child of light that is ever beautiful in the eyes of the Divine. As you make your way through this world, live in the purest love you can attain in this moment. Remember that the Creator and you are one; whatever kindness and grace you offer yourself (and others) you give to the Creator of all. Let conscience be your ally and love your finest truth.

Wednesday: Archangel Gabriel

True sight lives not in any physical sense but in the inner vision that connects to the Creator. Take a few moments to rest your eyes and tune in to a realm more profound that the one you see before you. Draw the pure essence of love and light into your being on each breath, and imagine yourself surrounded by light as if you stood at the center of Creation itself. Behold the magnificence and glory of Spirit. See beyond the senses. Here you may find wisdom and clarity and reveal the way forward. When you open your eyes again on the world of form, you may sense a glimmer of what exists beyond the sensory and find you have reawakened hope in your heart.

Thursday: Archangel Raphael

At the close of each day, find a gentle, safe space to land. Even if this remains out of reach in the physical world, you have the power to build that sacred place within your heart and soul. Imagine a glade surrounded by protective trees. Within this clearing, a soft, cool bed of moss beckons you to rest beside a bubbling spring that gently flows into a brook. Overhead, sunlight warms you by day, and moonlight caresses the senses by night. In this silken, sylvan realm, lay down your head and gaze toward the heavens. Reach out to the infinite, eternal essence that lives in all life, and sink down into the sustaining, soothing energy of the Earth below. Balance between the worlds, and let your being rest securely in the embrace of the Divine.

Friday: Archangel Uriel

As you grapple with the struggles of this world, you may lose sight of the power of Creator to resolve any situation. Live in the assurance that miracles abound in the divine embrace. Every instant, the Creator breathes into existence wondrous opportunities and marvels beyond measure or number. In the deep recesses of your heart, you know this to be so. Trust in Spirit. Regard whatever you face at this moment as a means of inviting in the power, love, and grace of God to provide the shift that is needed.

Saturday: Archangel Zadkiel

A kind of spiritual alchemy occurs when you focus on helping others. You may begin to transcend your own difficulties in the process. Direct your attention to those who cross your path. Offer any small blessing you can to each one. Some may be closed off to your kindness, yet your effort will be etched upon their beings and will begin to shift them toward grace if even a glimmer of hope remains in their hearts. Beyond the impact on them, you create a shift within yourself that electrifies your being. You build spiritual reserves with each act of kindness. Your soul becomes empowered to transform your life. By being someone's miracle today, you begin to rise into the life you seek.

Week 29

Sunday: Archangel Michael

In calm and silence, abide with the Light of Spirit. Restore yourself. Depleted energy may be renewed in the heart fires of God's Love. Seek through the sacred space within your own heart the doorway to the purest Flame of Creator. We are as one within the Presence. Let Love burn through the wounds of the past. Abide now in the heart light of divine love.

Monday: Archangel Jophiel

The bumblebee never wonders why she can fly. She simply does. She is a master flyer whose wings generate miniature whirlwinds that lift her miraculously and move her in any direction her instinct beckons her. Each day bumblebees go about their business, collecting the glorious sweetness of life and serving the divine design. They dedicate all their days to the splendid light of creation. Wherever you are right now, whatever you are doing, recognize that in some way you too are serving the cause of creation. Bask in the beauty of purpose, for you breathe that purpose no matter what role you currently play as surely as the bumblebee.

Tuesday: Archangel Chamuel

The rose of the heart never ceases to blossom. It never fades and never fails. Its sweetness lingers unaltered through all your days and experiences and the wounds of your life. If you feel you have lost touch with that precious essence, know that your soul holds the remedy. Call unto the Divine to wash away the density that appears to hide your heart song from you. Bring down the walls you have built from the bricks of fear.

Wednesday: Archangel Gabriel

In the quiet of mindful meditation, walk into the eternal sea. Let the waters of the ocean of light wash through your being to cleanse body, mind, and being of all that is less than pure harmony. Invite the endless waves of Creation to flow through the consciousness on all levels. Become one with the serene luminescence that ripples peace into your world. Bathe in hope. Know you are complete in oneness with the great I Am.

Thursday: Archangel Raphael

The spirit never ages. Your soul abides beyond time. Whatever changes seem to befall the physical aspect, the truth of your being remains unaltered. Tap into the eternal springtime of your soul, the spirit of youth and vibrancy. Let that pure wellspring of renewal flow constantly throughout your mind, body, and life. Accept that eternal season of splendor as your reality.

Friday: Archangel Uriel

Today, set an intention to walk in oneness with the light of peace. Carry that purpose prayerfully in your heart and mind as you move through the world. When you move consciously in oneness with peace, every footfall upon the earth imprints serenity, and each breath expands this gift into your being. So peace may linger in each room after you have gone and upon all hearts whom you touch.

Saturday: Archangel Zadkiel

Call on the loving core of Creation's Heart. Peer deeply into your eyes as you gaze in the mirror and speak to yourself these words of love: "I forgive every thought, feeling, word, deed, experience, infliction, affliction, and injury of my life. I forgive each transgression and all moments of fear expressed in its many forms. In oneness with the eternal love and power of Creator, I hereby transmute these densities from my consciousness and free my body, mind, and being of all that is out of harmony with love." By speaking these words each day with heartfelt intention in oneness with Spirit, you invite deep transformation and abiding love into your life.

Week 30

Sunday: Archangel Michael

Creator beckons you to honor the path you were called to walk. Surrender to the divine intention for your life. Trust that you will be blessed the moment you engage that path truly, fully, and with your whole heart.

Monday: Archangel Jophiel

Spirit's joy does not wait for the weekend, for special occasions or downtime. The joy that lives in your soul is available in every moment. Awaken that gift of jubilation. Become the sunshine of your spirit. Moods may come and go, but a deeper happiness lies within the heart. Tap into that eternal essence and carry it with you into the world.

Tuesday: Archangel Chamuel

In human terms, the word compassion means "to suffer with," yet divine compassion rises above this definition. It expresses the ability to feel with those who hurt while at the same time inviting them to lift beyond suffering. Angels see the path forward, the light within, and the gift of grace in every situation. To live the light of divine compassion, embrace suffering souls with understanding, love, and kindness, hold the vision of those dear ones moving past the pain and into joy, recognize the power and light within them to shift beyond their current condition, and hold the intention and prayer that each one may find the grace and the gift that awaits them.

Wednesday: Archangel Gabriel

The pure light flowing ceaselessly from the Heart of Creation offers sustenance to your soul. Sometimes it is necessary to clear internal and external pathways in order to embrace that supportive life force. Envision the cleansing essence washing through your body, mind, and being until all you sense is the flow of that endless light. Drink from the cup of life and remember your essence, forever wondrous and divine.

Thursday: Archangel Raphael

Seeing wisdom is not the same as being wisdom. A lesson is not truly learned until it is integrated. For this reason, often the same experience repeats multiple times over the course of one's life. Each occurrence offers an opportunity to incorporate knowledge and expand understanding. Recognize the wisdom gained from each experience and allow that insight to integrate into the psyche and deepen the perceptions. In so doing, you embark on a path of powerful healing.

Friday: Archangel Uriel

Your sisters and brothers of Earth are your traveling companions through life. Each one, no matter how blanketed in the density of shadow, is meant to be loved. Radiate so powerfully the love of Creator that you burn through the illusion and perceive the child of light within even the most seemingly lost souls. You are not asked to embrace them in their current state but to recognize that, beyond the dissonance in which they clothe themselves, a beautiful, cherished child of God longs to be free.

Saturday: Archangel Zadkiel

Life never ends. The universe ever expands and life shifts to higher frequencies. There truly is no death. Each child of light has a choice to give belief and sustenance to death or to life. The angels urge you to embrace life, to recognize that death is merely a part of the illusion of this world, and to live as though you were a miracle, for you are, you see. You are everlasting and glorious, as the Creator made you. Empower the miraculous.

Week 31

Sunday: Archangel Michael

Gentle spirit, know that there is always a hand to help you should you fall, a compass to guide you in times of fear, a shield to protect you amidst the chaos. You are loved. Let the angels who walk beside you light the path ahead.

Monday: Archangel Jophiel

Awaken the mind to the blessings of the heart! The surest way to remain aware of life's beauty is to evoke the wondrous, glorious wellspring of gratitude held in the heart and spirit. Look around at the beauty of the natural world. Feel the sunlight or the soft breeze on your skin; bask in the richness of sensory experience—the sights, scents, sounds, tastes, and touches of physical life. Discover joy in the camaraderie of kindred spirits. Behold the splendor of your own precious soul! Engage with life. And offer thanks to the Creator for these gifts.

Tuesday: Archangel Chamuel

Are you treasuring the love you receive each day? Are you accepting it with your whole heart, your complete being? Whether or not you realize it, the Divine blankets you in infinite love in every moment. Countless others—family, friends, animal companions, even co-workers who cherish your presence in the workplace—the many who share your journey and feel grateful you are in this world offer that gift as well. Consider this. Open your heart to it. Let your mind conceive of the prospect of being abundantly loved. Not everyone has the capacity to show you how much they appreciate you, but you are held in the hearts of more loved ones than you know. And legions of angels send you love right now. Breathe that in.

Wednesday: Archangel Gabriel

Angels sing in celebration of life, of all the boundless beauty of the universe, of the constant graces flowing forth from the Creator. Each sunrise and sunset, each moment of wonder beckons the angels to sing. Will you join the chorus of creation? Choose a song for each day to align with the joy or peace, the love or compassion, the grace or beauty you wish to behold in the world, and sing that tune with your whole heart. Sense the jubilation of song. Embody the joy of celebration.

Thursday: Archangel Raphael

The Divine seeks to relieve your burdens and invites you to take the first step by letting go of worry. Despite circumstances, your spirit recognizes that all is well. Your heart emanates this truth. Let the mind align with your finer nature. Speak sincerely to the Creator of all, "I relinquish all to You in the knowing that miracles abound through Your love. I gratefully place my worries in Your loving embrace and welcome the wondrous solutions Your infinite grace provides."

Friday: Archangel Uriel

Devotion cultivates miracles. Daily prayer and service to the cause of kindness nourish the soul and nurture blessings. Open the heart and mind each day by asking how you may assist the Divine. Live as a vessel of love and a keeper of peace.

Saturday: Archangel Zadkiel

What in your life needs changing? What do you seek to shift? Tap into the essence of transformation that lives in the heart and mind of Creator. It's always available to you. In your sacred heart, ignite the flames of transcendence. Merge the light of love and power, and set ablaze the patterns and programs of limitation and fear. Bathe in the spirit of possibility. Creation begins with your intentions and moves forward based on your actions.

Week 32

Sunday: Archangel Michael

Some may believe that power and love are two distinctly separate qualities, yet the two always exist as one within the Heart of Creator. Those who seek power for itself, absent of love, will never find grace or true joy. Those who pursue love without maintaining their inner truth lose themselves and lack balance. Power and love intertwined create a world of honor, kindness, and blessings. Seek the union of love and power within yourself in order to live in harmony.

Monday: Archangel Jophiel

Inspiration is written upon the wind. Its treasures lie waiting for you to appreciate the beauty all around you. Drink in the richness of Creation. Draw the waters of light from the infinite stream. Enliven the vision and allow the Creator, the eternal muse, to spark your gifts.

Tuesday: Archangel Chamuel

A circle of light surrounds you at this moment. Sense yourself inside that unbroken ring of love that never leaves you. Long before you took your first breath on this good Earth, you were born within the limitless, eternal, pure essence of Creator's heart light. You are forever a part of the circle that expands unto infinity. Your ceaseless soul invites you to remember that oneness. Speak this into your mind, "I am the circle of light expanding forever. I am ever in oneness with Creation's heart." Throughout this day, remind yourself as often as you need to that you are the circle. You have access to the infinite in every moment.

Wednesday: Archangel Gabriel

In every moment, you have an opportunity to serve as a divine messenger. Every word carries an energetic charge. When expressed with profound feeling from the heart and spirit, the expression "I love you" has the power to heal. Consider your words carefully today. Behold their power as you use them wisely and kindly. Embrace the ability to evoke feelings of joy and peace as you spread gentleness, grace, understanding, compassion, and love through your speech. You could be the difference someone needs to rise into their power and live their light.

Thursday: Archangel Raphael

Envision a field of green as far as the inner eye can stretch. Sunlight shines upon this unending emerald landscape. Breathe deeply of the vision before you. Visualize running free across this expanse like a child filled with joy. Here, in the space of healing, your true self—radiant, whole, and unencumbered by the burdens of your life—awaits rediscovery. Embrace this scene and this picture of yourself. Hold and expand it into your body and mind. Imagine you are this joyous, carefree child filled with wonder and glee. Set the intention to live as fully and jubilantly as the youthful version of you in this vision.

Friday: Archangel Uriel

A tone sounds throughout Creation that echoes the perfection of your unique being at the moment your spirit was born into existence in the heart and mind of the eternal. That tone carries the purity of your heart and the essence of your spirit. Every angel recognizes the music of your soul and senses when you shift more fully in tune with that song. This sound reverberates in the background all your days upon this Earth. Behind all the noise of the world, beneath all the layers of dissonance, this resonance plays without end. Listen carefully in your quietest moments. Listen in the peace of your perfect heart, and you may hear a fragment of a melody that expresses your wondrous soul.

Saturday: Archangel Zadkiel

Each soul aches to be truly seen. Go into the deep quiet beyond the reaches of the mind, and look at those around you. Peer into their eyes. Sense their souls. Just as you do, each one of your fellow journeyers offers a gift. Each one holds a sacred promise. In the serenity of your beloved heart, recognize the beauty of the people in your life. Many of them have lost sight of it themselves. Perhaps you have as well. The farther one strays from that true self, the more fear may alter the outer demeanor, yet the true self remains pure and precious. Gaze at what lies beyond the fears and the failures into the profoundly loving light of the spirit. If you can see a flash of the soul's truth, you can hold that reality for those most dear to you. Offer this same gift to yourself. Recognize the beauty of all.

Week 33

Sunday: Archangel Michael

Creator placed a compass within every heart to guide each soul onward toward light and love. The guidance of the conscious mind, which certainly can help in weighing options on the mundane level, falls short when it comes to discerning the truest path outlined by Spirit. You can never fail if you walk the path of your heart and soul. Even if you falter, you will always rise by staying true to this course. Listen to your heart each day and heed its wisdom.

Monday: Archangel Jophiel

Activate your inner child through activities that bring you joy. What sparked delight in your early years—reaching for the sky on a swing, playing in the forest, fingerpainting, singing? Why not take a chance on feeling that sense of elation again? Pursue the joyful you today. Yes, it's Monday and you may well have to go to work, but your time afterwards belongs to you. Today, give that time over to the child within who aches to play, pretend, and reclaim joy.

Tuesday: Archangel Chamuel

In the world right now, countless souls suffer in a myriad of ways. Their cries never go unheard. Their pain is felt throughout the cosmos as surely as is their joy. Angels cannot sink into the pain and still retain the pure essence of love, yet all angels can sense those feelings, embrace them for an instant, and transmute that hurt into love. Ask for help and it is yours. You simply need to rise to meet it.

Wednesday: Archangel Gabriel

Hope is no small thing. This divine gift has the power to draw the mind out of the stagnant spaces where only gloom and misery abide. Hope lives in the purest essence of creation and prepares the way for you to rise. It washes clean the fear that resides inside the baser aspects of being and allows the consciousness to focus on the desires of the spirit. Relinquish the worries of the moment and lift your eyes and heart in hope. This is the first step to creating a finer tomorrow.

Thursday: Archangel Raphael

The body remembers long after the mind has forgotten. The memory of past injuries, both physical and emotional, can linger in the corporeal form. Current aches may serve as a reminder to tend to your issues from the past. Ask yourself what lies beneath the present sensation. Become the explorer of your psyche. Seek the origin point of each present pain. Trust the answers your body gives you when you inquire about the source of physical disharmony. Take the steps necessary to let go of what was, embrace the wisdom of the experience and the teaching of those times, and embody a more healed and whole you in the now.

Friday: Archangel Uriel

Whatever is happening in your life today, take a moment to suspend the outer world, to hold intention, to imagine that you are touched by the Divine because, of course, you are. Breathe the purple light of transcendence, inhale the golden light of peace, and draw in the ruby light of passionate service. These three alchemical energies balance passion with peace, burn through detritus to illuminate your pure golden essence, and energize your highest intentions.

Saturday: Archangel Zadkiel

Will you live the light of freedom today—freedom from limitation and lack, from hate and fear, from judgment and unkindness? Perceive the invisible chains with which you have bound your life. In order to attain true liberty, you must relinquish the bondage of limiting programming. Imagine those repeated pathways of fear being set ablaze with divine cleansing light. Intend that you shift to a mindset of peace, joy, and blessings. Rise into the knowing of Creator's unlimited truth and powerful love. Recognize that you may align with all God's gifts and graces.

Week 34

Sunday: Archangel Michael

Believe in yourself and in the Divine. The universe paves the way out of darkness and into light. You are being guided to resolve the issues that trouble you. All the help you need is at your service. Call upon the Divine with your noble heart light, and all aid shall be given!

Monday: Archangel Jophiel

All souls long to sail upon the sunshine and waltz among the clouds, to flow upon the endless sea of joy and remember the days divinely cascading amid the stars. The angels whisper softly, "Even with your feet upon the ground, you still may hear the sound of wonder trumpeting its tune and join the dance of life's miracle." Sense yourself in oneness with all life, with every sunbeam and all the stars in the night sky. Your spirit will help you. This is your truth.

Tuesday: Archangel Chamuel

The child of light within you seeks solace and longs to rise beyond fear. The Divine sends you love to heal the wounds of your early years. Let the sadness and the pain and the patterns they created leave you now. The loving heart of Divine Mother can wash away your worries. Relinquish into her tender embrace all you have held and see your life begin to change.

Wednesday: Archangel Gabriel

Building a strong foundation for your life is paramount in walking the path of light. Many practices offer essential elements in creating a framework for a spiritual life: daily connection to the Divine through prayer, mindfulness, contemplation of the sacred, breath, intention, decreeing, and acts of kindness, charity, service, and devotion. Such a foundation provides peace, hope, and stability through life's challenges.

Thursday: Archangel Raphael

Join the call to Creator to bless all life, to heal every heart, to mend every broken soul. No gift is more sacred than to offer such prayers for all the kindred of Earth. Speak these words with the fullness of your heart: "May all the love I have ever known, all the seeds of light I have ever sown, every bit of grace I have ever shown now be magnified through the Heart of Creation to heal all life."

Friday: Archangel Uriel

What resonance are you sharing with those in your life today? What feeling are you emanating? Whether you exude peace or dissonance, you affect all in your environment. Plants, animals, minerals, humans—all life constantly absorbs and exchanges energy. Give all discord to the Creator for instantaneous transmutation into love. No matter how much sorrow or frustration you feel, the Divine can transform it, leaving peace in its stead. Breathe in harmony, love, and grace to take the place of that which you relinquish to God. In doing so, you bless all those around you.

Saturday: Archangel Zadkiel

Creator beckons you to rise beyond the illusion, to awaken to and live in divine reality here on Earth. This requires diligent discernment and placing the focus on the love of the heart and the wonder of the soul. Meet selfishness with unreasonable generosity of spirit. Face troubles with hope and faith anchored firmly in heart and mind. When the world around you appears in upheaval, bring your awareness to the sacred, the serene, and the ceaseless wonder of Creation. It is not possible to change the world profoundly without first aligning with the Light and stepping into a higher reality within one's personal perception. Find your sacred stillness and become the loving channel for peaceful transformation.

Week 35

Sunday: Archangel Michael

At this time, embrace deep cleansing for your entire energetic being. Thought patterns linked to past pain muddy the waters of life that flow to you. Allow the flames of the Sword of Light to engulf the detritus, the self-destructive and limiting beliefs and behaviors. Call upon Creator with a true heart and God will assist you.

Monday: Archangel Jophiel

Treasure the golden moments when the world sparkles in sunshine and light reaches into the corners of your mind. Walk among the beauty that surrounds you and remember you are a part of it as surely as every other luminous miracle of creation.

Tuesday: Archangel Chamuel

The greatest love of your life is the one and only Creator of all that is. Creator's Heart never wavers nor ceases in its perfect expression of purest love. The finest union you ever shall know is with the Creator when at last you return to the Alpha and Omega, the Aleph and the Tav. Nothing of this earth can match such unconditional, unblemished, infinite, eternal love, yet in every moment the Divine invites you to rise, to reach for that level of love. In so doing, you climb ever closer to a higher reality of love and begin to acquire the qualities of your highest self, and you inspire others to love with greater harmony and grace. Seek, then, the purest love your heart may hold.

Wednesday: Archangel Gabriel

Others seek your support and guidance at times of stress and need. Strengthen your reserves of light and life force so that you may provide a presence of wisdom, support, encouragement, and truth without taxing your personal energy. Remember to ask for the assistance you need. The Divine will be with you.

Thursday: Archangel Raphael

The angels hold your healing intentions with you. Focus the mind on the image of your life as you wish it to be. Color the consciousness with the vision of your wholeness, grace, and blessings. Amplify this visualization through the corridors of the heart and the pathways of love, joy, and gratitude. When opportunities to align with the vision present themselves, rise to the occasion and act on the synchronicity the Divine offers. In choosing this, you join with Creator and welcome the blessings God wishes to impart into your life and world.

Friday: Archangel Uriel

What majesty the canvas of your life painted with the sweeping brushstrokes of Creator's Heart and Hands! The Divine always sees the entire canvas colored in hues of beauty and radiance. The most splendid painting you ever have beheld cannot compare to Creator's vision for your life. Sometimes the journey seems circuitous, but in truth divine design lies behind every passage. Will you allow that gracious portrait to unfold divinely? Learn from each stumble, remain humble, and rise into greater wonder.

Saturday: Archangel Zadkiel

Close your eyes and imagine a glorious garden beyond any you have seen with human eyes. A pathway illumined in golden light winds inward toward the center of this sacred space. The flowers and trees glow with ethereal light and shimmer in radiant rainbows of color. You feel drawn along the path, moving effortlessly towards the heart of the garden. There, a serene pool sparkles from the light that shines down from above. Sit here in the silence for a span. Breathe out all you have been carrying that has felt heavy or burdensome. Let the light flowing from above encompass you and fill your being with a gentle, soothing essence from the Source of Creation itself. When you feel ready to depart along the pathway and return to your waking world, take with you the peace and the quiet of this garden.

Week 36

Sunday: Archangel Michael

It is time to bless and release thoughts and human programming which no longer serve your highest good. Limiting beliefs say to the Divine, "I believe that God's power is limited." Yet, the power of the Creator is infinite, and you exist within the Creator. Relinquish fear and limitation and embody faith.

Monday: Archangel Jophiel

Imagine you are a sunbeam shining alongside billions of others just like you, enlivening those who seek your gentle warmth, encouraging growth, bringing light to all the dark corners of the world. In a way, that's exactly what you are. You and all your companions across the planet have the ability to shine, to encourage, and to enlighten. You may have lost sight of this eternal truth, yet your spirit remembers for you. Connect to that knowing and radiate your warmth, your inspiration, your light to those around you. While you're at it, be sure to look in the mirror and offer these qualities to your own wondrous self.

Tuesday: Archangel Chamuel

A seeking that stems solely from the mind seldom reaches divine intention. Prayers travel most easily along the channel of love. Adoration of and deep gratitude to the Creator give your prayers wings. Ask the angels to amplify your love and join with you in expanding heart light as you pray. The answer to your prayer is expressed in the prayer itself when love and light accompany the words your heart gives voice to.

Wednesday: Archangel Gabriel

The constant motion of creation is ever expanding, yet its essence can best be accessed in the stillness. Reach into the core of your heart, the light of your spirit, and tune to the channel of love. Manifestation awaits you there.

Thursday: Archangel Raphael

A profound longing exists in every soul to experience oneness with the Creator. In truth, being separate from the limitless essence of the Creator would be impossible, yet the illusion of this world often clouds the mind and makes this deeper reality seem remote. Life on Earth allows the embodied spirit to experience the illusion of separation in order to awaken to the joy of reunion. The Divine invites you to expand your spiritual awareness and restore the sense of connection that your spirit already knows. Seek the solace of the Sacred Heart, the point within you where the spirit anchors in oneness. There, you begin the journey back home.

Friday: Archangel Uriel

Honor the light and the life granted to you by the Creator. Live each day, each moment with passion. Let the flame of your spirit guide your life. When you are truly engaged in the act of living passionately and powerfully, all things become possible, all blessings manifest in harmony.

Saturday: Archangel Zadkiel

Amid the shifting sands of ephemeral life, cultivate the swift return to center no matter what situation arises. Develop your inner awareness of any fluctuations of energy and emotional resonance you encounter. When you experience turmoil in the face of an outer challenge, seek to discover the deeper cause behind the inner turbulence. If you are willing to face the issues that linger within the consciousness, perhaps from childhood or adolescence, you have the power to overcome reactivity and embrace spiritual stability. When you sense inner disturbance, ask yourself what lies behind your distress, how to heal and clear the root cause from your being, and how to shift from a reactive emotional condition to a responsive spiritual state. The spirit never falters nor experiences chaotic conditions but rather acts with conscience, wisdom, and love. When you have reached the next level of consciousness evolution, you will do the same.

Week 37

Sunday: Archangel Michael

The strength at your command streams forth from a limitless well of divine light. You are being empowered to generate the gifts of wholeness and blessings you seek. Drink deeply of God's Love and be blessed!

Monday: Archangel Jophiel

Dive into joy at least once each day and sustain that feeling for as long as you can. You may find it among the simplest moments—while holding your child or caressing your animal companion, while spending time with a loving friend, in the glorious radiance of sunbeams or the glistening dewdrops catching the morning light in your garden. You may discover it in the flower that rises through a crack in the pavement or in the smile on the face of a passing stranger or perhaps even in the long-anticipated completion of a task. Look for those moments and expand them through your mind, heart, body, and being. Joy is a subset of God's love and light. Live it as often as you can.

Tuesday: Archangel Chamuel

Seek your spirit family. Create your circle of kindred souls. Find those who walk in peace, who are guided by the heart song, who honor the Earth and her children, who rise into hope and desire to support their fellow travelers. Your spirit will guide you. Approach life with an open heart and honorable intentions, and these relationships will unfold. Develop these profound associations in order to build community and shift consciousness to a more loving, aligned aspect. This unity of spiritual kindred provides a strong foundation to move toward a finer reality.

Wednesday: Archangel Gabriel

Your spirit is in complete oneness with the Divine. So it has been and so it shall be evermore. Breathe grace and love. Let the Light circulate throughout your being. What you seek flows to you on God's breath even now.

Thursday: Archangel Raphael

What if everything your heart desired and your spirit supported already existed just one step ahead of you? So much is waiting for you just around the next bend in the road. So many blessings, including some you have not yet dreamed, lie on the horizon. If you are too busy contemplating your troubles or focusing on your pain, you may miss the signposts that guide you to the very gifts you seek. Raise your gaze to the glory that awaits. Lift your heart in grateful song. Remember you are one with the infinite and align with the truth of your light.

Friday: Archangel Uriel

Those who learn to see with the heart and perceive with the spirit may transcend the visible and behold the wonders of Creation. Outside the realm of human perception lives a world beyond imagining, the space where all things are possible and love creates miracles. The angels invite you to journey there. With practice, profound intention, and deep connection to Spirit, you may discover how to peer behind the curtain, see through the veil, and walk in kinship with the invisible realms.

Saturday: Archangel Zadkiel

Do you hear the calling deep within—sometimes a whisper and sometimes a resounding signal—drawing you toward your divine dream? In whatever way that unfolds, take a step today toward your truest path. Pray for direction. Tune in to your inner knowing. Seek through means both spiritual and tangible. The closer you come to moving with the flow of your spirit's call, the more fulfilled and blessed your life.

Week 38

Sunday: Archangel Michael

Free will is a gift that comes with great responsibility. Acknowledge that you decide how to live your life. Your thoughts and emotions build the future. Accept this responsibility each day by choosing to expand joy and love and to transmute fear and limitation.

Monday: Archangel Jophiel

Where the mind sees ominous gray skies, the spirit perceives the potential for rainbows. The spirit always peers beyond the illusion into the beauty beneath the surface. May you rise into divine perception and recognize the bud of grace ready to blossom, the glorious moment just a breath away, the wondrous blessing awaiting your awakening. Can you sense the sunlight shining when it isn't visible? It is, you know. It's shining just for you—right now. Feel this. Call to your waiting soul what will brighten your life today.

Tuesday: Archangel Chamuel

All blessings flow from love. Every gracious gift is a tributary formed from the great sea of love. The qualities you most prize—joy, peace, grace, abundance, wonder, beauty—all are born of the supreme gift of Love eternal and limitless. Whatever you encounter today, do your best to live in the sparkling heart and arise into love. You may just change the world.

Wednesday: Archangel Gabriel

Only love may conquer fear. Only light can dispel darkness. The angels stand with you in this time to conceive a compassionate future. Despair dissipates in the face of hope. Failure transforms into renewal. Every moment you spend contemplating peace, love, grace, and blessings lifts the whole of humanity. Look to the Light and live as an emissary of Creator on Earth.

Thursday: Archangel Raphael

Just across the channel of forever, all those you have ever loved whose light has passed beyond these shores abide. Your beloved pets and your closest kin await reunion in the timeless world beyond, where for them a mere blink of the eye has passed since you and they stood together on this Earth. What they would tell you now is to delight in each moment of your earthly life—the times of pain and of joy—for they are all a gift beyond your imagining. Even though the realms of light hold wonders as yet undreamed, your physical life exists as one of God's greatest miracles. Each instant is an honor, each circumstance a great teacher. Drink it all in. Give thanks for every rising and setting of the sun, for you are blessed more than you know.

Friday: Archangel Uriel

The sun still shines every bit as brilliantly when thick clouds block its light. The light of your spirit still radiates its glorious essence even when shadow fills your mind and obscures your vision. You are more luminous than you could ever know and more wondrous than you can yet perceive. Sometimes others may sense your light when you have lost sight of it. Look to those, both divine and human, who remember your truth when your radiance remains hidden to your mind. When you lose your way, fill your world with kindred spirits who will always remind you of the light within.

Saturday: Archangel Zadkiel

Someday in the distance, perhaps not so long from now, you will travel at the speed of love. This is the greatest universal constant as yet unmeasured by mortal minds and perceptions. You can conceive of and gauge the speed of light as you recognize it, but the rate of divine light and love remains a mystery to the third-dimensional observer. Know that love and divine light travel instantaneously. The moment you think of someone and expand the feeling of love to them, they receive that blessing. No construct of time can measure how swiftly a loving feeling can travel from one part of the world to another. Angels stand outside time and radiate endless love in the myriad of frequencies created by the infinite Source. With intention and open-heartedness, let your imagination step into that endless knowing where such love lives. Sense the everlasting love and the instantaneous transmission of divine grace. Then recognize that this is the truth of your own being as well. Be the love, the light, the transcendent power of peace.

Week 39

Sunday: Archangel Michael

In each moment, in absolute love, the angels gratefully honor the will of the Creator. What a gift to surrender all in service to the Divine! Each time you choose to yield all that you are to divine will, you open to joy, love, and blessings beyond imagining.

Monday: Archangel Jophiel

Will you serve as someone's beacon today? Along with all of your fellow sojourners through life, you travel toward a shoreline you cannot see and need a light to guide you onward. Divine love and light shine effortlessly like a guiding star in the distance. May you always recognize its glimmer through the fog of illusion and the appearance of separateness. And may you always return to love and turn its essence both inward and outward to expand grace into this world.

Tuesday: Archangel Chamuel

Someday the armor around your precious heart will fall away. You had countless reasons for guarding that part of you in a world that seemed achingly treacherous. All the hurts and sorrows bound you in the defenses that kept both the danger and the love at bay. The pure love that naturally emanates from the sacred heart in so many has been locked in a protective encasement. But the walls will come down. Today may be the day or tomorrow or in some unexpected moment when that beautiful heart expands its light so brilliantly that nothing can withstand its immensity. The ocean of love will pour forth through the crevices, and then every defense will burst its seams. The tide of love can only be held back for so long. This is the truth of things. And that most gracious gift will flow in both directions until all the wounds you have lived through heal. The tidal wave of love is coming.

Wednesday: Archangel Gabriel

What wondrous blessings the Light brings into your life! The treasures of the spirit by far surpass the trappings of the material world. The true self within you longs for the graces of the eternal. Be assured they are yours already. The spiritual gifts ignite as you shift your mindset and attune to a higher reality. Imagine the Spirit surrounding you with purest light and love. Enliven the soul fire of Creator's splendor and infinite glory! You live in the God stream of that perfect life essence. Tap into it and realize your dreams.

Thursday: Archangel Raphael

The Earth is a part of the infinite, eternal, benevolent Light of Creation. This wondrous planet constantly processes energy. That which is out of alignment with divine resonance is transmuted and shifted out of the earthly body. Humans are meant to learn this practice as well. It is one of the most vital parts of the healing journey. Recognize that each issue that arises in the physical realm holds a frequency that urges you to identify the deeper meaning, accept the teaching of such an experience, and shift both mind and body to a more harmonious resonance. The spirit of Earth and of the angels will aid you in learning this practice.

Friday: Archangel Uriel

Great blessings occur when you consciously align with the rhythm of life. Creation comes with a burst of energy, yet in its wake lies the peace and stillness of the eternal. To begin each day, tap into the flow of creation, which exists in all life and streams constantly from the core of the universe. That current of creative light shall carry you through the day. After the creative energy disperses through daily activity, tune in to the setting sun and sense the moment that night falls upon the earth. With it, the quietude of serenity embraces all who take the time to perceive this shift. When you align with this rhythm, allowing peace to calm the mind at the close of the day, you embrace restful sleep and prepare the physical aspect for resuming the rush of life that returns with the sun.

Saturday: Archangel Zadkiel

The old programs of your life no longer function ideally, for they were never meant to last. As you transmute the painful restraints you have placed upon yourself, you start to recognize that every situation can be transcended in one way or another. The power of transformation lives in your heart and spirit. Unlock the mind and relinquish limited thinking. When you surrender to the spirit the restrictive thought patterns you have formed and align with the higher mind, you begin to rise into a limitless mindset.

Week 40

Sunday: Archangel Michael

Your spirit summons you forward. The angels hold a flame before you to light your way. Envision the path ahead glowing in golden-white light. The purpose of your uniqueness is encoded into your soul. Access your destiny in the essence of your spirit.

Monday: Archangel Jophiel

When you encounter the dark clouds of density and dissonance in the world, call upon your inner reserves of pure light, and remember that your spirit holds only lightness of being. The shadows that fall in your life can remain merely for a season. Your soul incorporates and integrates only light and grace, benevolence and peace. That which is less than love can never truly be written into your consciousness nor your eternal being in any real sense. View them as what they are, mere illusion born of fear, and call upon the pure eternal essence of your spirit to see you through the darkened landscape of the psyche and the material world.

Tuesday: Archangel Chamuel

Such depth of love abides within your heart. In the realms of light, you existed as pure love. You are here on the Earth to learn to love unconditionally as a human. Share love with all you touch. Open fully to love within your own life; cherish your spirit and all souls as the Divine cherishes you.

Wednesday: Archangel Gabriel

Life weaves through all existence in an unfathomable tapestry of infinite proportions. No single individual can comprehend the enormity of Creation, yet the limitless mind and heart of the Creator holds the entirety of existence in the most loving embrace and pure, omnipresent consciousness. You may never have the full vision of your unique expression of life; you may be unable to discern even your own "big picture" in its fullness. But you may trust in its divine unfolding and connect to the light of your spirit for guidance as the fabric of your own life is woven thread by thread. Attune to the nuances, to the movements of energy, to the signs and messages divinely sent each day. In doing so, you rise into that vision held by your own soul and your Creator.

Thursday: Archangel Raphael

Your rhythm and bearing affect your wellbeing more than you know. When you tread heavily and move with shoulders slumped and eyes downcast, your inner being shrinks and you fall into a gait of gloom. When you walk with the cadence of the spiritual child of light you are—light-hearted, stepping cheerfully as if ready to skip at any moment, honoring each step as a grace and a gift, your entire being expands and celebrates. Your physicality affects your mentality just as your mentality affects your physicality. The very atmosphere around you will begin to shift as you carry yourself with childlike jubilance. If you are physically incapable of such movement, then recognize that the inner self, which remains unaltered by physical challenges, has the power to convey the same expansive, light-hearted, glorious resonance. Lighten the heart, illuminate the mind, lift the spirits, and the world around you transforms to meet your inner gait of grace and joy.

Friday: Archangel Uriel

Despite life's many occurrences, your light remains unchanged. The real you never fades, diminishes, nor alters. Your immutable and unwavering spirit radiates the purest light of the Creator from an endless wellspring. Remember this as you face challenges or circumstances that appear defeating, and let this truth bolster you. Your inner reserves of light may be called upon any time your human resources seem to fail you, for there is no end to the blessed brilliance flowing forth from Creation's Heart.

Saturday: Archangel Zadkiel

One of the most essential gifts you may offer yourself is that of forgiveness of all who have crossed your path in an unwelcome way, of all painful experiences, of all that has ever transpired in your life that left a mark of sorrow or anger. Until you truly, deeply forgive, you retain an energetic entanglement with all of those individuals, situations, and feelings. You may remain tied to the circumstances you wish to shed and often draw similar ones into your life. Until you relinquish the fear frequency through forgiveness, you remain enmeshed with those souls who have wounded you and those experiences that have pained you. Freedom lives on the other side of profound forgiveness. You already know this deep within. Let yourself dive now into the well of forgiveness for all in your life.

Week 41

Sunday: Archangel Michael

You have encountered many lessons in this life, often repeating the same ones. Rather than viewing these as a burden, your spirit asks you to consider them an opportunity. Each one offers a gift that may be beyond comprehension in the short term but will become clear once you have mastered the challenge and moved on. Believe in the strength the Creator offers through your own spirit. Know that you can graduate beyond whatever issue you currently face and need never confront it again if you are willing to embrace and embody the lesson and rise into a deeper understanding.

Monday: Archangel Jophiel

The little ones can still hear the song into which they were born. They often sense and see the angels lingering nearby, those who served as spiritual doulas ushering their pure, perfect souls into this reality. As they grow older, discover the tangible world, and learn human language, the memory of that soul song often fades. The farther they stray from the moment of innocence, the more distant that melody becomes. When someone behaves in a fashion that is out of harmony with the light of the spirit, it is because they have completely lost touch with the song of the soul. Divine utterance has been blocked by the shadows and traumas of their earthly life. In such cases, seek to forgive and pray for their rising into love, for there is no greater loss than the connection to the spirit. And if ever you happen to catch a tune playing in the back of your mind, something you cannot recall having heard, hum along with that melody long forgotten and remember who you are.

Tuesday: Archangel Chamuel

If you had any idea how many kindred spirits existed in the world, many not far from your very door, you would never feel alone or lacking for connection. In order to find your spiritual family, you must shine the light that is uniquely yours. So many just like you seek other souls to form bonds of community, to lift each other on the path of light, to honor both your oneness and your uniqueness, and walk side by side into the great unknown, co-creating in kinship as you go. If you hide your inner truth and conceal your precious light, those whom you may aid and those who may offer you a helping hand will remain at a distance. Spirit invites you to take the risk, to let others see you, to radiate your glorious essence, to find your circle, your kindred, your family.

Wednesday: Archangel Gabriel

The world outside holds many fascinations and obligations that call to the small self, yet your spirit belongs to something far greater than these. Make space in your life today to seek the sacred within. Find those moments of grace that exist forever in the loving presence of the Creator. When you take the time to free the mind of constraints and open the focus to the limitless essence of the spirit, the world around you takes on a different tone, and you begin to view all in life as part of the sacred and eternal.

Thursday: Archangel Raphael

The treasures of the spirit are endless and myriad. Your soul has access to all that serve your purpose and highest good. You need only tap into the flow of such blessings, attuned to the frequency of love and joy, take the steps to live your light, and welcome the gifts and graces you seek to further your vocation and honor your journey. Envision yourself already on the truest path of divine service and trust that the road shall reveal itself.

Friday: Archangel Uriel

Some who walk the path of light may feel at times as if you must inch your way through a strange, treacherous landscape where pitfalls may arise at any moment. Do not lose sight of the truth that you came into this life with the tools the Creator gave you, which means you have been prepared since the beginning. Each day, journey within into the place of peace or rise into your spirit and commune with the eternal light that is your truth. The more you connect to the spiritual essence, the stronger your consciousness becomes. When faced with the chaos of the outer world, you may access the reserves of your inner being—pure love, peace, harmony, grace, forgiveness, and faith—to face whatever lies along the path. Allow the feelings you encounter to pass through you, washing them in your perfect light, and know your peace shall deepen as you practice aligning with your soul.

Saturday: Archangel Zadkiel

Build within your being the bonfire of Creator's boundless love and transmuting power. Place all your worries and difficulties into that conflagration of divine transformation. Imagine sending each one of your concerns directly into those sacred flames of forgiveness. Inwardly, see or sense every one of those problems being consumed by God's grace. When all have vanished, call forth the gentle rains of mercy and freedom to flood your life with blessings and envision the miracles you wish to receive. Let love, light, and peace reign supreme in your heart.

Week 42

Sunday: Archangel Michael

Rest now, child of light. You so often serve as both protector and caregiver for others. Breathe and take respite in the embrace of the Light. Recognize that you are never alone as you fight the battles of your life. Give yourself the time and tenderness that the Divine gladly offers in every instant. Regain your center and remember that you are not the only guardian soul to look after your loved ones. Legions of angels come now to give you aid.

Monday: Archangel Jophiel

Have you forgotten the joy of play and the marvel of viewing the world through a child's eyes? When challenges arise in your daily life, allow your internal processes to work on them while you abide in the now. There will be time for brainstorming, deliberating, and mental gymnastics, but sometimes the best solution comes after "recess." Step outside routine. Walk into wonder. Leave worries for another moment. Stretch your ethereal wings and waltz to the music of the universe for a span. When you return to the task at hand, you will feel renewed, and the answers may just come to you as if whispered by angels into your bright spirit.

Tuesday: Archangel Chamuel

The greatest service—in reality, the truest calling above all others—is to love. If every soul honored that one highest purpose, the world would be filled with beauty, grace, and joy. It may not always seem convenient or easy when those around you behave in ways that test your resolve. But your spirit has the power to love all life. When you lose patience or falter on the path of love, cede command to the light of your soul, which always works for the Creator. The small self may feel challenged, but nothing can oppose the light of Spirit.

Wednesday: Archangel Gabriel

Oh, the glory of the universe and the splendor of each unique spirit woven together into the grand design! To behold the wonder of even a single life is to view the majesty of Creation's finest miracle. Have you forgotten that you are a marvel? The angels remember and stand in awe of the perfection of all of God's creations, including you. On those days when you become caught up in the tumult or lost in the rush of life's challenges, call on your angel guardians to hold the vision for you of the beauty of your soul, the light of your being, the wonder of your existence. And find the place of stillness, even for a moment, to peer into the invisible and witness the great tapestry of your life from a higher perspective. Try to see yourself through divine eyes for an instant, beloved one, and let joy fill your heart.

Thursday: Archangel Raphael

You've seen pictures of the Earth from above, that shining blue planet with its soft white clouds. Countless angels work tirelessly to honor life in this world and hold all in the healing hands of the Creator. Will you serve as an Earth angel today, offering solace to your fellow travelers and love and blessings to the world of animals and plants? Recognize the spirit within each one, the beauty of all of God's creations, and hold them in the most loving regard, for they and you are a part of the Creator. Cherish the butterflies and bees, the birds and beasts. Write upon your heart a love for all that God has made, and, if you are willing, bless this blue and green planet with all your might and recognize the interconnectedness of all life.

Friday: Archangel Uriel

Savor the uniqueness of the moment. You may be the solitary soul seeing a sunrise or sunset from your position, the only one who glimpses a rainbow in that interplay between sun and rain, the single person who notices that glorious reflection of clouds in the puddle beneath your feet, the sole individual who experiences an instant of beauty the likes of which no other has known. The Source of all life gives these moments to you freely. You may feel drawn to the window at the perfect second or awaken 10 minutes early just so you will be there to view wonder unfolding. Such priceless gifts exist just for you on any given day. Look for them when your spirit guides you to such treasures, and drink deeply of the grace offered. Let it linger in your consciousness for as long as you can hold it.

Saturday: Archangel Zadkiel

Consider the true nature of your being beyond the physical. You are far more than matter. The density through which you often must wade amid the turbulence of the world may affect the temperament and, if allowed, even interact to a degree with material substance, but your spirit remains untouched by all except the Light. For this reason, the angels invite you to attune to the soul, to the infinite and pure. That which seems insurmountable to the physical aspect and to the human conscious mind holds no sway over the ethereal. Your spirit knows beyond doubt that anything is possible when you align with the perfection of the spirit and allow an energetic shift to alter the seemingly tangible world.

Week 43

Sunday: Archangel Michael

Constantly Creator speaks to your heart and soul and seeks to uplift you from the mire of misery or the cacophony of chaos. Spirit says, "When you are lost, I will find you. When you struggle, I will be your balm. When you feel sorrow, I will embrace you. Wherever you are, I am with you." For those who have bypassed challenges and already risen to a space of inner peace, know that you are held also and invited to offer to others the gifts with which you already have aligned.

Monday: Archangel Jophiel

Yellow rays of sunlight illumine your being whenever you share the gift of jubilation. Laughter and smiles hold greater importance than you may realize. These blessings enliven the spirit and banish fear. How long has it been since you felt exuberance so exhilarating that your being radiated joy? A bright golden-yellow flame lives in your heart waiting to expand such joy into your being, to remind you why the angels sing and how wondrous life is. Tap into that flame. Rediscover elation wide enough to fill the world. Today is as good as any other day to begin anew.

Tuesday: Archangel Chamuel

An ordinary day sometimes takes on extraordinary characteristics. An influx of love washing through the mind, body, and being can awaken the miraculous. How many serendipitous moments have passed without acknowledgment? Today, imagine that every drop of sunshine is made of tiny cascading streams of divine love and light. Watch for the sparkle, the glints of luminosity, the glorious elements that come when the heart is open and the mind is willing. Follow the guideposts that lead to unexpected wonders. You know, miracles happen even on Tuesdays.

Wednesday: Archangel Gabriel

Your life is not meant to be an endless procession of struggles. Your light exists within the greater whole of Creation, one forever with the infinite Creator of all, who experiences life through you. What would you desire for your beloved Creator today—challenges, tedium, pain, or perhaps peace, love, and joy? No matter what exists in the outer world, you have the one and only champion you will ever need, God. Every issue in your life can be shifted in less than the wink of an eye. Perception is everything. Believe and perceive according to the choice of a single moment. When you are ready, you will understand.

Thursday: Archangel Raphael

Wanderers through the world, you traverse deep crevices and climb rugged mountains, seeking always to renew the spirit and honor the path. Through darkened corridors or sunlit byways, know that your course remains steady and true. Your sails shall fill with the winds of glory to guide you onward. You cannot become lost unless you cede your path to shadow. You, dear journeyer, have countless kindred to lift your eyes back onto the trail of light. No matter how far afield you may seem to have traveled, trust that Spirit will lead you in the direction you need to go. If the pathway has seemed circuitous, you simply have been given abundant opportunities to learn along the way.

Friday: Archangel Uriel

You were born to manifest the glorious, unique radiance Creator expressed through your soul. When you allow yourself to shine, you offer to those around you and to the wider world a gift that no one else may impart. It may take time and courage to rise into your inner truth and honor your calling. Rely on the Divine to bolster you as you share your light.

Saturday: Archangel Zadkiel

The eternal law of forgiveness shines into every heart seeking redemption. The grace that flows from that forgiveness can shift lives and transform the world. Surrender your heart to true forgiveness. Relinquish the blocks of the mind that hold mercy at bay. You and all others deserve the gift that surpasses all save love itself. The waters of mercy run deep, for this is no shallow experience. Dive into them as often as needed, and prepare yourself for the change that comes when the depths have been reached and the blessing is complete. Be willing to alter your perceptions, erase your barriers, and rebuild in the name of all that is holy and blessed the life of true freedom.

Week 44

Sunday: Archangel Michael

You are more than you know. The power of the Light flows through your soul. Divine strength infuses your being. Lift your gaze from the melee to the spirit. Become the inspiration you were meant to be. Honor the truth of your soul.

Monday: Archangel Jophiel

Diminishing thoughts do not serve the Creator. Whether directed toward the self or another, limiting, doubt-filled judgments and fearful "what if" scenarios only strengthen that which is less than love and light. Before the blemish of a world addicted to lack and limitation, a child's imagination embraces the wondrous as reality, the miraculous as actuality. The unlimited mind recognizes the vastness of possibility as reachable. That child's consciousness sees and believes what most adults seem to have lost: the mindset of miracles. It is time to stop giving credence to the lack and limitation you see before you and remember you are a child of God and, therefore, beyond such constraints. Fuel your imagination. Reignite your belief. Rise to the occasion.

Tuesday: Archangel Chamuel

What sweet elixir the heart holds! The threefold flame of Creator's power, love, and grace call to the consciousness to serve as a means of shifting your world toward blessings. Do not let these energies of divine alchemy wither within you. Expand these sacred flames as needed each day. Awaken the golden-white flame of wisdom, truth, joy, and grace when you need guidance or inspiration. Claim the power of the blue flame when you require clarity or protection or hold the desire to fuel for your purpose. When you seek compassion, harmony, or love, call to your pink flame to magnify these feelings within yourself and magnetize your being to draw these gifts to you.

Wednesday: Archangel Gabriel

All souls are intended to emulate the ever benevolent, glorious Creator. All were given the gift of creation, yet few use it consciously and wisely. Call to Spirit to purify your intentions, to clear your pathways of thought, emotion, and creation, to bring your being, even on the human level, into alignment with divine creation. Haphazard thoughts and thoughtforms muddy the energies within and around you. Take the time to cleanse them daily. Cultivate the conscious awareness of the mind's energy and direct your focus, light, love, and spirit toward solving rather than creating issues. This task requires diligence and perseverance, but the result shall be the transformation of your life and your world toward blessings for self and for all.

Thursday: Archangel Raphael

Mental agility and tools, learning, and knowledge are valuable gifts to be sure, yet these pale in comparison to the treasures of Spirit and the graces of Creator. The mind must become the servant of the heart and the spirit. Attune the psyche to the soul, the mindset to the mindfulness of spirit. Rewrite the patterns that no longer serve your highest good, and install new ones that energize your life with the grace of the Creator. Through prayer, intention, mindfulness, meditation, conscious cleansing of the mind with Creator's light, re-establishing pathways of harmony, and other means, you may shift the mental aspect into its truer position—no longer the ruler of random thoughts but rather the servant who honors the divine wisdom of the spirit and the heart.

Friday: Archangel Uriel

Rejoice in the knowing that your radiant spirit, ever united with the infinite beloved Heart of Creation, knows the answer to every problem and concern. Your heartfelt prayers communicate instantly into the spirit that surrounds you and anchors within you. Your every desire is written upon the eternal Heart and Mind of God. All prayers that cause no harm to self or others and are aligned with your most beneficial journey live already in the ethers, awaiting your readiness. You are the one you need to convince of your value, your belief, your deserving nature. Creator already knows how worthy and wondrous you are and awaits your alignment with these truths.

Saturday: Archangel Zadkiel

Altering one's life takes a moment of powerful choice followed by the necessary steps along the path. Select the patterns you wish to imprint for the betterment of your life and the world around you. Inscribe them upon the heart and mind daily. Actual change requires willingness, commitment, dedication, and energy. Take mental, emotional, physical, and spiritual steps toward the results you seek. When you reveal to your spirit the deep desire to transform your life through intent, initiative, action, and alignment, you notice the results swiftly. How long does it take to rise to the place you wish to be? An instant or an age? That remains up to you.

Week 45

Sunday: Archangel Michael

Avoid judgments of self and others when you see the world or your own life out of balance. Instead of recriminations, seek your center; embrace that power and love in your own heart. Trust in the truth that all will be restored. Creator's Power and Love will align all in the moment of readiness.

Monday: Archangel Jophiel

Between the earth below and sky above, a world of wonder awaits your discovery. Seek the places that nourish your soul—the cascading ocean waves that wash the psyche in serenity, the woodland spaces where tall trees settle and soothe the senses, the untouched corners where adventure lies waiting, the sunlit pathways where you may bask in renewing warmth. Escape the mundane even for a few minutes a day to reclaim your spiritual connection. Such moments revitalize and restore your communion with Spirit.

Tuesday: Archangel Chamuel

Poetry and music aligned with the heart nurtures the soul. At their finest, these are much more than entertainment. They awaken the divine spark and aim the awareness toward wonder. Whether writing, reading, or listening, attune to the lyrical gifts that feed your spirit, align your consciousness, uplift your psyche, and enliven your heart. These graces in the form of words and music open channels for light and love and color the perceptions with beauty.

Wednesday: Archangel Gabriel

What if the Creator depends upon you and your kindred of light who walk the Earth to dream a finer reality into being? Would you lift your awareness to the heights and anchor within heart, mind, body, and soul the vision of the divine dream? The journey begins when you connect to Creator's dream for your life and move into alignment with that glorious version of reality. The more fully you realize your own path, the greater your desire to enrich the lives of all your fellow travelers. Join with your kindred, each honoring purpose, and build the radiant, blessed tomorrow for all.

Thursday: Archangel Raphael

Each child of light is born with the gift of healing. When your little one places a hand over an injured knee, she or he reveals a deep, abiding knowing, perhaps on an unconscious level, that God's Light can work miracles, even through the hands of a child. Creator's radiant heart is always available to those who believe in it, and its power is boundless. Is it time to regenerate your healing gifts?

Friday: Archangel Uriel

Shine a light into those dark corners of your psyche, those forgotten places where hurt and fear linger. See or sense the wounded child or youth who cowers in the hidden spaces. That part of your consciousness needs grace, courage, and love. Within your sacred heart, all three traits await your readiness to bring peace to that once injured aspect of your being. First, send the soft, gentle, nurturing pink light of love to illumine that part of you. Let its warmth and tender compassion soothe you. Next, extend the golden light of grace and joy to offer the most profound healing and remind your wounded self of what is possible. Finally, surround that part of you with the empowering blue light of courage that protects and shields the innocent and restores faith. Invite that part of you to join you in the present, to heal fully, to feel loved and safe, to embrace grace, and sense the strength of divinity ushering you forward along the path.

Saturday: Archangel Zadkiel

Faith and love unite in the gift of mercy. So often you have offered this gift to others but withheld it from yourself. You, too, deserve your compassion, understanding, and clemency. The Creator forgives all who seek with an open heart and a willingness to change. Nothing is beyond God's ability to wash clean. Call on the Divine for aid as you free yourself now of some long-held shame or wounding that prevents self-love and self-worth. Wash in the violet waterfall of divine mercy. Let its light flow through you. Allow its love to grant you liberty from the self-judgment you have clung to for so long, that has inhabited your mind and kept you from fulfilling your promise.

Week 46

The angels love rhyme and often communicate through its cadence. This week, I share their words of love through verse.

Sunday: Archangel Michael

What lies hidden shall be revealed. What lies broken shall be healed. Let the true Light be your shield. All in shadow soon shall yield, for Creator's Love you wield.

Monday: Archangel Jophiel

Your heart holds the key to wisdom within, to what is and what has been. Remember Spirit is your friend and love abounds without an end. Your glorious and gracious soul already lives within the goal.

Tuesday: Archangel Chamuel

Softer than snowflakes settling on the ground, angels brush past without a single sound. Only with the heart can they truly be heard. Your eternal soul can discern every word.

Wednesday: Archangel Gabriel

A whisper of stardust, a song of flight, a forever angel shining day and night, a luminous soul eternally bright—such is the truth of your eternal light.

Thursday: Archangel Raphael

When gratitude sings in the soul, your heart can reach its highest goal. Your life held in eternal hands brings to fruition divine plans.

Friday: Archangel Uriel

Within your heart the light of peace ignites a flame that shall not cease. Its gifts of grace fill every space that your mind may dare to embrace. Its song can open heaven's gates and wash the world of fear and hate. So with your whole heart radiate the purest peace you can translate.

Saturday: Archangel Zadkiel

May freedom live within your soul. May love divine make your heart whole. May pure light on you ever pour. May your spirit ceaselessly soar.

Week 47

Sunday: Archangel Michael

Do not shrink from the power of Creator's Love. Do not hide the light of your own spirit. Speak these words into your mind, heart, body, and being: "I am constantly empowered to make the choices that most align with my wholeness, vibrant health, infinite joy, unending peace, and all gifts of light and love. I accept these blessings and extend them through harmony and divine love to all others."

Monday: Archangel Jophiel

Take the time to embrace your child (both inner and outer). If you have no offspring, lovingly hold the inner child you once were. Children, no matter their age, seek approval, affection, assurance, and kindness. Pledge your unending love to the child within. Express your eternal affection for those you parent. Either way, the gift is the same. Teenagers may roll their eyes and pretend your words provoke embarrassment, but internally another story lives within their hearts and minds. They ache for that gift of grace your words speak into their psyches. Whether young or grown, let your children know how much they matter to you. And allow your inner child to feel safe, cherished, and heard. Live this every single day until your heart and theirs, your mind and theirs, feel deeply secure in this truth.

Tuesday: Archangel Chamuel

There are laws that govern the universe on many levels, but all others fall under the greatest one: the law of love. Deep within, you know this truth: God is Love. To love is to serve the divine cause of love. To offer love without expectation or limitation is to emulate the Heart of Creation. The small self tends to place restrictions upon love because of life's wounds and subsequent patterns of self-protection. You are meant to shed these patterns and restore the profound gifts of love as years pass and wisdom is gained. Seek the path of eternal love and restoration of its purity.

Wednesday: Archangel Gabriel

Every angel has a mission to fulfill. For those in the realms of light, that purpose is unending. It may shift location or manner at times, but the assignment remains unaltered. A creator angel creates. A protector angel protects. A healing angel heals. And so it is. You, too, have a mission and within your spirit all the tools and graces you need to bring it to fruition in this world already exist. You may need to relearn them, but the way already lives within you. Let the white fire of creation awaken your knowing and kindle your desire to fulfill the course the Creator has set for you.

Thursday: Archangel Raphael

Be gentle with yourself and those around you today. Some hearts are tender for reasons unknown to you. Your own heart would welcome the soothing essence of kindness. There are times when work pulls you away from the more important task of offering benevolence, understanding, and compassion. Perceive the needs both within and without, and honor the call of your heart to act with thoughtfulness and grace, mindful and aware of the power of words, kindness, and empathy.

Friday: Archangel Uriel

Write this blessing upon your heart and mind: You are a radiant being of love, light, and peace, ever expressing the grace of God here in the world of form. You are the eternal light of spirit into which you were born. Honor the power and passion of your heart, live the light of your soul, and cherish the mercies and gifts Creator offers unto you. Recognize the riches of your truest self, blessed beyond measure in the fullness of your being.

Saturday: Archangel Zadkiel

Wield the power of Creator's decrees. Open your mind to the Light of Spirit and invite God's grace to be expressed through your words. The creative aspect of your being welcomes the opportunity to give voice to the Light. Allow the words of love to flow from your soul, and write in language that speaks to your intentions and beliefs the declarations of divine truth that live in your spirit. For example, you may wish to say, "I am forever in oneness with the Light and Love of Creator," or "I am the infinite flow of God's graces into my life that I may in turn share these with all life." Let the framework fit your purpose aligned with Creator's will, and you cannot go wrong. Breathe light and begin.

Week 48

Sunday: Archangel Michael

Spirit always serves as your safe haven. Lean into the wings of light and love that enfold you in divine embrace. Anchor the infinite universal heart light into which your soul was born. Rest secure in the knowing that you are protected. Find your truest home in the sanctuary of the soul.

Monday: Archangel Jophiel

Unending light streams through the universe into every particle of existence. The more light you absorb and integrate, the more you shift in frequency and become aware of spiritual consciousness. When divine light interacts with density, which must be released and transmuted in order to rise beyond the framework of fear, energetic storms occur. Your heart and soul seek ever to lift into a higher resonance of peace and joy, but the mental constructs that serve the old patterns of fear struggle against the incoming pure essence of love, and you experience turbulence. Such conditions persist only as long as the old programs remain. Seek, then, to shed the patterns of the past and relinquish to Creator all that no longer provides assistance to your psyche.

Tuesday: Archangel Chamuel

Will you become someone's proof of love today? One or more individuals of great heart but equally profound loss may cross your path on any given day. More than anything, such souls need to be reminded that someone cares, that they do not walk alone, that the Divine still stands with them in their hour of need. As you reach out with your kindness and love, you will spark within them that truth, lift them into knowing, and give them a moment of precious unity with the greater whole. In the process, you will offer all these things to yourself. You, too, shall remember that you are not alone, that you are loved, that indeed love is all that truly matters in this world and throughout the universe. In the act of giving it away, that love will return to you beyond limits.

Wednesday: Archangel Gabriel

When a soul leaves the cradle of Creation's Heart to be born into earthly life, countless considerations and arrangements come to pass. Despite preparation and the wondrous gifts bestowed, complete understanding of what it is to live that impending life remains unknown. In the realms of light, unborn spirits know infinite grace and see the perfect resolution to every challenge that may arise. Their clarity and purity of being prevent the deeper comprehension of the element of fear, the physical response, the tangible perception of life. Until earthly life commences, much remains beyond the full perception that exists amid perfection. Knowing this, be kind to yourself when you falter or give in to the illusion so rampant in this world. Seek guidance and wisdom from the Creator through the light of your spirit. No matter what you encounter, trust that you remain within the purest essence flowing from the Heart of Creation, and have faith in God's grace to guide you.

Thursday: Archangel Raphael

When you seek to heal, remember the interconnectedness of all aspects of being and all forms of life. Your mind affects your heart and body, and the same is true in reverse. Your spirit houses all facets of your being and holds the keys to healing every one of them. Part of the healing journey is to honor and address the need for healing on all relevant levels. Your spirit knows the ideal course to follow. Call on the light of your soul and on the Creator to powerfully energize all measures you employ for healing, medical and holistic, to free you of this imbalance.

Friday: Archangel Uriel

Your immortal soul invites you to anchor God's blessings in your heart and translate them to your mind. No lack exists in the pure essence of Creation. The part of you that remains in conscious oneness with the eternal recognizes this truth, but human programming and patterns of thought and behavior may block the light of Spirit like dark clouds obstructing the sunshine. The sun remains behind those clouds, and some light gets through, but the world takes on a lackluster tinge when gray blankets the radiance of the solar orb. When shadows seem to block your eternal sun, the light of the spirit in constant oneness with Creator, you may falsely perceive a scarcity of blessings when, in fact, such graces and gifts abound. Rise beyond the gloom into the light that awaits your rediscovery. Hold yourself in the golden beams of infinite blessings. Let this essence saturate your consciousness and carry that light back into your mind to revitalize your path.

Saturday: Archangel Zadkiel

All blessings flow from love in its myriad of rainbow light. That love expressed through the violet ray flows as forgiveness. Mercy is the rain gently quenching the thirst of the parched earth. It is the sunlight warming the skin of a frozen world. When you truly train the mind in the ways of forgiveness, a path known fully by the heart and soul, you may feel a kind of rebirth. So powerful and gracious a gift cannot be reserved for the few who seem to deserve it. When you come to experience the full benevolence of spiritual forgiveness, you will want to share it with all, no matter how profound their transgressions. To truly live in the similitude of the Creator is to offer such mercy as God offers you.

Week 49

Sunday: Archangel Michael

Every prayer lives in the Heart of Creator. Hold your truest desires within your own sacred heart, and fan the flames of God's power, love, and wisdom within. Let the Light sustain you in trust so complete that you exist in knowing: All shall be well. Blessings shall flow. Faith and gratitude open the path to answered prayers!

Monday: Archangel Jophiel

Every thought transmits a frequency and carries the potential for greatness or its reverse. Those stray flashes of insight that march through the mind unbidden may be the saving graces of your life. Those careless judgments that etch patterns in the psyche may exacerbate an existing issue or align with unforeseen consequences. When the angels invite you to live consciously and move mindfully through life, it is because thoughts matter more than most realize. Their weight increases when emotion attaches to them. They can change the world in whichever way you direct them.

Tuesday: Archangel Chamuel

No gift offered from the heart is ever too small to place before the Creator of all life. All the gold, silver, and riches of the world mean no more than the gratitude you pour into your prayers at the end of a day. Never look down upon yourself for what you feel is lacking within you. Focus instead on what you have to give. Your love remains the finest gift of them all. Creator sees you trying, knows your heart, and welcomes your prayers with the most open heart of them all.

Wednesday: Archangel Gabriel

Remember today that every word you express embodies a harmonic. Every syllable communicates a frequency. Will your words build beauty and wonder? Will your words speak into the heart and mind of God what you actually desire? When you choose to speak consciously, you build the template for your life upon a foundation of love, peace, and empowerment. The angels invite you to rise into conscious communication today.

Thursday: Archangel Raphael

What if the Creator smiles upon you today? Consider this. In truth, the joy expressed at the moment your spirit was birthed in the Heart of Creation still echoes through eternity. The smile never ends. Whatever you have done, you remain that child of light whom God loves boundlessly and eternally. Will you live that truth today? Will you shine and share the love of your soul with all life? As you do, you become the miracle you were meant to be.

Friday: Archangel Uriel

Sing to the glory of Creator. Sing of the peace that lives beyond all challenges. Intone the prayers of the ages and anchor reverence for all God's creations. Raise your voice above the cacophony and chaos of the mind and the outer world. Lift your utterance to express the fullness of your love. Let the song of your soul resound through every particle of your being.

Saturday: Archangel Zadkiel

You have been told many times to set free those you love so they may return of their own accord. In truth, you can never hold that which is not your own being. Those who share your journey serve as teachers, companions, guides, students, comrades, beloveds, and kindred. They were never held in bondage; therefore, it is not your place to set them free. All souls must do this for themselves. Your gift to others and to yourself is to find liberty within your being and live that truth that others may know it is possible.

Week 50

Sunday: Archangel Michael

Become the phoenix. Arise from the ashes of past wounds and difficulties. The power of God's love floods your being like the phoenix fires. It is time for rebirth and renewal. Let the Creator empower you to secure your wholeness and honor your truth.

Monday: Archangel Jophiel

Do not wilt before the tasks at hand. You have an inner flame that guides your life and fuels your creations. You have access to the eternal, unending love and grace of the Creator. Nothing can defeat your indomitable spirit. Whatever challenge you face, know in every fiber of your being that God is greater. You will rise to the occasion because you are not alone. You never were nor will you ever be.

Tuesday: Archangel Chamuel

You may have encountered situations in life that broke your trust or your heart. In such moments, you may well have built defense mechanisms and boundaries around the heart. But this is not your truth. As these barriers begin to melt through the power of Creator's love and your willingness to move beyond the old wounds, your heart will rise anew into a higher level of love. Someday, when you have dissolved all the defensive patterns and allowed the barricades to fall, the sacred heart will overflow its confines and fill your being with love and grace.

Wednesday: Archangel Gabriel

What is written between the lines of your life holds more importance than you may realize. When you tell your life story, you may focus on the grand brushstrokes, the accomplishments, the battles fought, lessons learned, and challenges embraced. But God lives equally in the small, ordinary moments that anchor your reality day by day. Every hug, each kind word, every hand on the shoulder of someone in need, every nuance of tender inflection, every time you emblazon life around you by singing with your whole heart in the shower or the car, all the belly laughs and outrageous giggles, every occasion when you pick up after your loved one without complaint, every doodle in the margins of life—Creator lives in them all. You live there too. Of those small moments, a life is built, a world is created, a miracle comes to life.

Thursday: Archangel Raphael

If one lives long enough, grief finds and breaks open the heart. The outpouring of love through the power of tears may seem overwhelming in such times. In those moments, the angels wrap your being in wings of light that express the pure love and comforting essence of the Creator. Consider this: Tears serve as the vehicle for release of powerful emotions that otherwise might enflame the consciousness and hinder the health of the body. Allow yourself to claim release, to relinquish the pain, and prepare the way for restorative grace and healing to flow. Invite all angels of light to assist you in the process and recognize the love remains long after the physical presence has departed this world.

Friday: Archangel Uriel

No matter the pain of loss, love remains alive and stays with you through life. Those long gone from this reality remember and cherish you. They invite you to hold the moments of joy, let go of the regret, and embrace the blessings of fulfillment that come when your heart heals enough to continue. Death truly is nothing more than a gentle passage beyond the boundaries of the physical. It holds no sway beyond the moment. Embrace life with passion and peace in the knowing that you live and carry into the future the precious essence of what once was.

Saturday: Archangel Zadkiel

Imagine yourself in an amethyst garden surrounded by shades of purple and violet beneath sunset clouds that filter soothing hues through the atmosphere. Saturated in these colors, you rest in the solitude of silence. Take yourself into this space within the light of your spirit. Bask in serenity. Return to your center, grounded in peace, anchored in the still point. Invite the light to wash through your mind, your body, your being, to clear the pathways of thought, emotion, energy, life. Such moments renew the spirit and refresh the mind and body. Return to this space of quietude and grace often to allow yourself respite and reconnection to what matters.

Week 51

Sunday: Archangel Michael

Fear serves no purpose in your life now. You are being asked to have complete trust in the power of the Divine to solve all problems, heal all issues, and provide for all your needs. Arise from what was and become your true self.

Monday: Archangel Jophiel

When you lose your footing or become lost in the shadows of this world or encounter another soul who has stumbled or fallen into the abyss, cling to the loving light that somewhere still exists within your own being or the ones who have wandered into the depths. No matter how far from the spirit someone has traveled, no matter how lost in the darkness, the Creator still sees the precious child of light within, crying out for deliverance. Remember the pure essence of that divine child that once you were or that other soul was. Imagine and hold the vision of rising for self and for all.

Tuesday: Archangel Chamuel

Your ancestors bestowed upon you more than the color of your eyes and other physical features. You stood witness to their failures and their finest moments. In so doing, you received a great opportunity: to shine as they shone and to rise where they fell. Consider the choices you have made based upon the values instilled either by alignment with what you saw as blessed or by opposition to what you perceived as profane. Every moment of their lives served as a teacher for how to walk in the world or how not to. The beauties they shared and the lessons they taught, both by example and by expression, informed your life in countless ways. Honor what speaks to your soul. They were part of your journey. Accept the wisdom that came from your lineage while rising into the full flourishing of your unique spirit.

Wednesday: Archangel Gabriel

Sing out the pure essence of your heart to the infinite, eternal Light. Creator does not care if you can carry a tune. Intone the melody that comes to you, and let it ring out your love to all creation. Allow the words to rise within your mind and give them voice with all your might, or you may sing to the Creator, "I will sing to You; I will bring to You all the love within my soul. Let me live Your grace and bring to this place the love that makes us whole. May I live Your Light every day and night so that I fulfill my role."

Thursday: Archangel Raphael

"Thank you" may seem the simplest expression, yet when it comes from the heart, it holds more weight than a thousand lesser phrases. To feel genuine gratitude is to align wholly with the Creator's blessings, to embrace the gifts offered unto your soul, and to express the truth of your willingness to receive them. Always say these words with the fullness of their meaning. Give them the energy of your heart. Let them rise from your lips to the heavens above, to the totality of life, to the Heart of Creation. In so doing, you awaken to greater levels of love and truth and empower the path before you with these graces.

Friday: Archangel Uriel

Sacred ceremonies honor life's passages and the Creator's presence within them. At every seeming ending and new beginning, during each potent moment of meaning, these observances bring you into alignment with your inner truth and your place in the moment. Showing reverence for the Divine within all brings one closer to Creator and builds a bridge and bond with those who share the journey with you. Is it time to initiate such a ceremony in your life?

Saturday: Archangel Zadkiel

Liberty begins in the spirit, emanates its light through the soul, and translates to the mind, which may reject or welcome true freedom by clinging to old patterns or relinquishing and rising beyond them. Often, the choice lies hidden behind the murkiness of fear in its many forms: pain, anxiety, blame, anger, hatred, and shame among others. All are based on past events and retain only the level of power you are willing to feed them from moment to moment. Creator wishes nothing more than to release you from the bondage of such patterns, yet only you can choose to surrender them for transmutation into love. If these pathways and programs are deeply etched into the psyche, you may need to make that choice many times until you are sufficiently ready to truly, powerfully, permanently relinquish that which is less than love. When you are, call on the Divine to aid you as you take that first step and the step after that and all the others that follow toward a more fully realized life. The angels are here to hold your hand as you march forward resolute in your determination.

Week 52

Sunday: Archangel Michael

Expansion of the Light flows into all existence. You are a part of that flow—infinite and multi-dimensional. Some part of you is forever sharing the light of healing, the message of truth, the wisdom of divine grace. All that you have ever been, all you are now, and all you ever shall be remain as one. You can be no less than what you are. All else is illusion. Become your soul's truth, and you will share every aspect of light the Creator shines through you.

Monday: Archangel Jophiel

You will always come unto the fountain of joy along the path of love. There is no other route, you see. More often than not, the path reveals itself through the open-hearted giving of love. The more fully you move into compassion and kindness, the more swiftly you will find your way to that spring that ever flows with golden liquid light to quench any thirst of the soul or the psyche. Once you find your way there, run like an eager child toward that fountain and drink until your mind and heart feel the lightness that comes with such radiant joy.

Tuesday: Archangel Chamuel

What if love held no boundaries? What if it flowed infinitely without qualification or condition? What if a miracle lay waiting in every shining particle of love? Someday you will see the truth that all these things are real, that every moment there streams love beyond your imagining, expanding forever throughout the universe. When your mind is quiet and your heart is open, you may sense that stream. Even as it is filtered through the density that surrounds you, this light never ceases. You will find your way through these times. You will walk again in the pure essence of love that even now lights the path before you.

Wednesday: Archangel Gabriel

In the deep and quiet places, the Light whispers your name. Amid the noise of this world and the chatter of the troubled mind, you may not hear the gentle voice that rises from the stillness, yet it is always present. Set aside precious moments each day to listen, to deepen the connection to your spirit, to turn the dial of your mind to the channel of love, peace, and unending light.

Thursday: Archangel Raphael

Look around you at the beauty of nature. You may detect divine design in so much of what you see in the natural world—the arrangement of flower petals, the patterns of pine cones, the spiral of seashells, the formulation of tree branches, even your own DNA molecules. The Creator asks you simply to discern what is clearly present and discover the truth hidden in plain sight: you are a part of the grand design, the wonder of creation, the glory of God. You belong to the infinite and are an eternal flame within the great universal mind and heart. Today and every day, to the best of your ability, live the Light of the Creator. Live fully and beautifully, for every moment resounds in the Heart of God.

Friday: Archangel Uriel

Walking the path of peace requires steadfastness. When you view eruptions around you, especially when they are aimed toward you, the familiar response is to react in a similar vein. Only when you hold the spirit close and deeply anchor the Light of the Creator can the purity of the heart triumph over the temptation to lash out. Those who choose to rise along this pathway of serenity and reverence understand the need for daily communion with that which is holy, blesséd, and pure. The lamp was lit long ago to guide you along this journey. Even in the thick shadows that seem to permeate this world, that light remains, unwaveringly drawing you onward. Trust the truth of your spirit. Reignite the lantern each day. You shall never walk alone.

Saturday: Archangel Zadkiel

The embrace lives in the letting go, and the letting go lives in the embrace. Always the beginning holds the ending within itself, and the ending recalls and honors the beginning. Even the stars live out a cycle of wondrous illumination until their fuel is exhausted. But no star ever truly dies nor does any form of life. They become a part of the universe in a different way. Even now, countless stars that sparkle brilliantly in your night sky have already completed their cycle and united with the Creator in the eternal dance of the cosmos. This is never a sad occasion. Their light lives on in countless ways and shines forever in the Eternal Heart and Mind. For those stars, it is merely returning home. Remember this. Life may change; your world may transform, yet it shall never die.

Archangel Exercises and Meditations

These techniques are intended to bring you into deeper alignment with the specific archangels and also with your own spirit and the Creator of all. Each one begins with a prayer. (Please use whatever name for God fits with your own beliefs.) You may wish to record the meditations for greater ease.

Michael: Archangel of Divine Will, Purpose, and Protection

Oh, Archangel Michael,
Shield me with the power of God's love.
Connect me to my truest purpose
That I may dedicate myself unwaveringly
To serving Creator's eternally gracious will.

Meditation:

Prepare yourself and the room where you will meditate. Light a candle or use another means familiar to you to bring a sense of the sacred to your space. Call on the Creator and on Archangel Michael in whatever way honors your beliefs. You may include words to this effect if you choose:

"I call upon the holy eternal Light of Creator and the blesséd Archangel Michael to stand with me now, to surround my being and my home with your purest protection, and to wash clean all within and around me and this space that is less love and light. I lift my voice to the Heart of Creation and ask for your aid now."

You may listen to beautiful music (without lyrics preferably) as you breathe deeply, imagining that each exhale carries out all worries, fears, and detrimental thoughts and energies for instantaneous transmutation into love and that each inhale draws divine light and love into your being. Simply breathe light for at least five minutes. Doing so generally allows the body to relax and the mind to release concerns and extraneous thoughts. If your body continues to feel taut, you may gently stretch and continue to breathe. If the mind refuses to quiet, then simply allow the thoughts to pass through you without focus or recognition.

Envision yourself inside a white spotlight streaming down from above you, flowing from the highest point of your spirit, bathing you gently in a glow both soft and powerful. Imagine a brilliant, blazing blue-white flame of energy beginning to descend around you as the presence and pure essence of Archangel Michael enters your space. Soon you become engulfed in a pillar of blue light that pours through the top of your head into the entire physical body and expands outward to fill the space around you. The blue flame feels warm, gentle yet mighty, and deeply reassuring. For some, it may even feel like home. Invite Creator's cleansing energies to flow throughout your mind, body, and complete being and cleanse all that is out of harmony with your purpose, your path, your true self, and your loving light.

In this state, you may call on Archangel Michael to assist you in whatever ways honor the path before you and trust that he and his angels will come to your aid.

When you feel ready to end the meditation, give thanks to the Creator, to Archangel Michael, and to your own beloved spirit and bring your awareness back fully into a wakeful state.

Acts of Beneficence Aligned with Michael:

1. Archangel Michael, protector of the innocent and those in service to the Divine, welcomes the assistance of human helpers. Be present with those who have been discriminated against or treated unfairly. Offer a listening ear, a helping hand, an encouraging word, or a strong shoulder. When finding the right words seems impossible, simply allow your heart to speak in silence, emanating love, empathy, and understanding. Stand with and walk beside the innocent and injured souls in need of justice and aid. When facing the specter of injustice, seek to lift the oppressed and downtrodden.

2. Endeavor each day to act with honor, speak only truth (kindly, of course), and behave fairly to all. Serve as an example of integrity, hereby inviting others to live in the Light. Let every word and action reveal the principles of your spirit.

Jophiel: Archangel of Wisdom, Illumination, Joy, and Inspiration

Oh, Jophiel,
Awaken joy within my soul
That the child of light within me
May shine more fully the light I am.
Illumine the path before me,
Let the wisdom of Spirit inspire and guide me
Unerringly
To fulfill my most gracious role.

Meditation:

Call on Creator to surround and fill you and your space with protection and grace. Imagine your conscious self, your mind, is a ball of light housed in your brain. Pray, intend, and imagine that this sphere of energy, your conscious essence, lifts gently through the top of your head and rises to about arm's length above your body, entering into a glowing orb of pure golden-white light. This radiant orb shines as brightly as the sun itself. Here, you feel safe and loved and inundated by brilliant yet reassuring light. Gradually, your inner senses acclimate, and you distinguish a pathway within this space. You discern it more with each passing moment and begin to walk slowly along this golden-white path toward a glorious garden filled with verdant growth, magnificent blossoms, and soft, peaceful energy. Your sense of harmony and centeredness grows as you move into the garden. A bright yellow sun shines onto all present in this place. You feel its warmth as you move along a circular trail toward the center of the garden.

Once you arrive, you come upon an eternal spring shimmering in the sunlight. A bench awaits you beside the waters, beckoning you to stay and rest for a while in this sacred place. Even though you may not recognize your surroundings, you find yourself comforted by a sense of the familiar here. You hear a soft, almost imperceptible sound just beside you as Archangel Jophiel's luminous presence alights next to you. His smile beams joy into your mind and heart. You may speak to one another or simply remain silent in the reverie of this moment. Bask in the memory of your spirit's joy. Recall that this is where your truth lives. Imbibe the glory of true grace, and set the intention to carry this light back with you when you leave this garden.

After you spend as long as you wish here, give thanks to Jophiel and to the Creator of all for the gift of this moment, follow the circular path back out of the garden, and imagine your consciousness descending back down the short distance to your body, entering through the crown chakra, and returning to your physical experience.

Connect again to the earth beneath you. Become aware of your physical self, but realize that glowing golden-white light now washes through you to help you remember your spirit's truth of joy.

Acts of Beneficence Aligned with Jophiel:

1. Jophiel is deeply connected to assisting children and the inner child to find inspiration, joy, and renewal. Many adults have let the issues of childhood plague and define their lives and have lost touch with the wondrous gifts that come when experiencing childlike innocence and jubilation. Many of the challenges we face now stem from

the wounds of the children we once were. Jophiel invites us to engage in joyful activities that help to heal the inner child. Swinging on a swing set, finger painting, using Playdough or Slinkys—all of these childhood activities and many others can awaken the inner child. Allow that child you once were to come back into your life, be heard, find ways to heal, and become a vital part of your life here in the present.

2. Call on divine inspiration and engage in creative activities that will bring blessings. If you don't think of yourself as creative, recognize you may simply have been trained to believe in a limited idea of what creativity is. Every person is a living expression of the Creator and, therefore, cannot help but be creative. Certainly, you can learn and use more traditional forms such as art, photography, poetry, collage, sculpture, or writing, but these are not the only means of embracing divine inspiration. Anyone can make a vision board or create a collage. Each time you put your own spin on a recipe or brainstorm with a friend or colleague who needs a solution to a problem, you are exercising your creative self.

You may access inspiration for anything from creating a business plan to building a sand castle to constructing a crystal mandala. Jophiel will joyfully assist in awakening the creative flow and tapping into the energy of inspiration. If what you choose to create helps others, you'll find the light of invention is always on.

Chamuel: Archangel of Divine Love, Charity, and Compassion

Oh, Archangel Chamuel,
Open my heart to Love,
Clear away the wounds of the past
And all that impedes the flow of blessings
Until I am one with Love Divine!

Meditation:

Call on the Feminine Divine, your own spirit, and Archangel Chamuel to embrace you in a protective bubble. Connect to the flame of love within your heart. Imagine a beautiful pink flame rising and expanding through your being, especially into the mind. This light of love and divine nourishment opens the path to blessings. Envision that loving light encompassing your being, filling every particle with love, awakening your consciousness to the truth of your oneness with all life. Visualize whatever aspect of the Divine Feminine resonates with your beliefs. This could be Archeia Charity, Chamuel's feminine counterpart, Mother Mary, or any other feminine presence of light. Imagine being embraced by a mother who loves you unconditionally and purely. She gently places her hand upon your heart and invites you to let go of all the wounds you have experienced in life. You lean into her embrace and allow all the hurts of this life to pour out of you, being instantly transmuted by the profound love of this beloved aspect of Creation's Heart. Let yourself be held for as long as you need, simultaneously letting go of the pains of life and drawing in the healing nourishment of love. When you are ready, give thanks and release unto the Light all you have let go. Breathe in the soft, pure essence of love divine. Bring the pink flame back from its expanded state into your sacred heart space. Become aware of your physical being and the space around you, and affirm this new state of love you are now ready to live.

Acts of Beneficence Aligned with Chamuel:

1. Perform acts of charity at least three times each week. These may be small offerings such as a pat on the shoulder of someone who needs one, a kind word to the grocery store checkout person, or any conscious effort to offer compassion. Giving does not always have to be financial. Often, the best gifts are those that arise from the heart.
2. Practice seeing the true beauty in yourself and others. Fill your heart with love as you gaze in the mirror or look at a loved one. Recognize the beauty that lies beyond the physical aspect, the pure essence of Spirit that lives in all of us. Inwardly repeat, "You are a being of love and light. You are beautiful and ever loved."

Gabriel: Archangel of Annunciation, Purification, Hope, Harmony, and Creation

Oh, Gabriel,
In your purifying light, I bathe myself.
With your clarity, I embrace harmony
Consciously
So that God's guidance becomes
My practice for this day.

Meditation:

Call on the Creator to place you and your space within a forcefield of perfect protection. Imagine yourself surrounded by a sphere of white light as you breathe deeply of that luminous energy. With each breath, pray and intend that you are breathing purifying energy to clear the mind and wash away all frequencies of disharmony. (Because white light contains all colors within the spectrum, be aware that you may inwardly sense other hues.)

Imagine a soft, liquid white light pouring from above you. As it flows gently over and through you, it carries away thoughts, feelings, and energies that no longer serve your highest good. They begin to melt and evaporate as this soothing light floods your mind, body, and being. Envision a wondrously beautiful angel alighting within the space just in front of you. Smiling, the angel asks for your hand. As you hold it outward, the angel places a gleaming white pearl in your palm. This pearl carries a gift from the Creator intended just for you. It may hold the answer to a prayer, a gift of clarity and harmony, a message of love and light, or an awakening to your divine dream—whatever is needed. Give thanks to this angel messenger and to the Creator for whatever blessing flows from this moment. Basking in the love and gratitude you feel, say farewell to this messenger of light. Breathe deeply. Trust that the pearl is held by your spirit and will come into your conscious awareness at the ideal moment. When you are ready, open your eyes and ground yourself. Once again, give thanks in the knowing that all will be revealed divinely.

Acts of Beneficence Aligned with Gabriel:

1. Sound the horn of hope in the lives of those around you. Seek to lift the downtrodden and to lighten the path before them by lending kind words and helping hands in any form that is needed or appropriate.
2. Practice looking beyond the conflict you see in the world and holding the light of harmony wherever it is most needed. In addition, when we dissolve discord in our own lives, allowing ourselves to move through anger or disagreement to recognize others as our kindred, we take a vital step toward shifting the collective.

Raphael: Archangel of Divine Healing, Service, and Divine Knowledge

Oh, Raphael,
Within your nurturing embrace, I place myself.
With your healing breath, I am joyfully renewed.
In God's grace and love,
Consecrate me to divine service.

Meditation:

After placing yourself and your space in divine protection, breathe deeply and slowly, listen to melodic, instrumental music (perhaps with binaural beats to induce theta state), and relax as fully as you can. Imagine yourself walking along a lovely path surrounded by trees and springtime foliage washed in sunlight. You come upon a glade and find a beautiful pool of serene water. A green glow radiates from its depths.

As you call upon Archangel Raphael, the waters stir and ripple briefly and then become calm again. If you wish to do so, you may wade into the pool and even immerse yourself in those gentle green waters. Raphael's soothing light surrounds you. Allow your stress, discomfort, fear—all that you carry that is out of harmony—to ooze out into the water. You may sense a dark inkiness leaving your body and mind. Release any concern about muddying the pristine waters, for the emerald pool instantly clears whatever you pour into it.

Allow the waters of the pool to help you relinquish whatever you no longer need. As you float in the pool, Raphael's presence becomes apparent at the water's edge—glorious, shining, and brilliant but equally serene. You see that he holds toward you a radiant chalice of liquid emerald light. You walk smoothly through the water or swim to where Raphael stands, and he hands you the cup. If you choose to, you may drink deeply of the elixir of wondrous light and allow its warm, nourishing energy to fill your body and your being. Every part of you feels soothed and comforted. When you are ready, you walk out of the water. Raphael wraps you in his wings of pure emerald radiance and guides you back to this space, to your body, where you return feeling nourished, loved, and restored.

Be sure to connect to the earth and drink some water after your meditation journey.

Acts of Beneficence Aligned with Raphael:

1. Because Raphael helps us dedicate ourselves to service, seeking a means of serving the Divine by assisting others brings us into greater kinship with this archangel. Your service can be any path you feel drawn to walk in the light. It may be helping older adults, caring for the young, visiting the invalids to bring cheer and companionship, feeding the hungry, volunteering at your church or community center—whatever you feel best suits your talents and personality. Raphael helps us strengthen relationships and deepen friendships, so sometimes service relates to being there for those closest to us.
2. Move through the world in a heart-centered way, showing kindness, gentleness, and care to all those you encounter. Bring spiritual nourishment to others by revealing the Creator at work through your own loving acts, words, and kindnesses.

Uriel: Archangel of Divine Radiance, Peace, Transcendence, and Devotion

Oh, Uriel,
In your light of peace, I place myself,
Accepting God's transcendent grace
Gratefully
So that I may minister and be ministered to
In alignment with Universal Good.

Meditation:

Rise early just before dawn on a clear day and find a safe haven where you can watch the sun peek over the horizon. Facing east, slowly breathe in the light of dawn. As you draw in the radiance of the rising sun, imagine it flowing through your body and mind. As the magnificent colors of peach, orange, gold, and lavender stretch into the sky, breathe them into your own being. The soft colors may soothe and harmonize your mind while the vivid, bright hues energize you for the day.

Bask in the radiance and know that this moment holds the potential for a powerful shift in your psyche and your life. Set your intentions and express your desires through prayerful meditation. Welcome Creator's Light to awaken the possibilities for fulfillment of each of these. Give thanks in the knowing that this or greater still flows now into your life.

If you wish to incorporate a specific breathing technique, you may use this one: The Radiant Breath.

1. Breathe in divine radiance on your in-breath (count of 8 or whatever is comfortable).
2. Circulate the radiance within as you hold the breath (count of 8).
3. Breathe out gratitude to the Divine on your exhale (count of 8). Exhale completely.
4. Pause in the place of emptiness and stillness (count of 8).
5. Breathe in divine gifts and blessings as you inhale (count of 8).
6. Hold the grace within as you hold the breath (count of 8).
7. Breathe out to expand your gift into the world (count of 8).

Repeat this three to six times. After the breathing exercise is complete, focus your awareness on the earth below you. Let your awareness sink into your feet, into the ground, deeply into the planet in order to center yourself in the physical body to continue your day. When you are ready and your feet feel steady, go ahead and move into your usual routine.

Acts of Beneficence Aligned with Uriel:

1. Perform a daily peace prayer and/or meditation for peace. Align as deeply as possible to peace within yourself. Call on Archangel Uriel and the Creator to anchor peace within you. Ask Uriel to carry to the Divine Heart the most fervent prayer for peace you can express. Give thanks and affirm it is done.
2. Volunteer to perform some form of ministering service at least once per week. This can be going to visit an elderly person, connecting with a friend who needs someone to listen, etc. When you do this service, radiate love as consistently as possible to those whom you are helping.

3. Practice regular devotion by selflessly praying for a specific person or group of people and holding the vision of wholeness, healing, peace, or other blessings (whatever is needed) for them for at least several minutes. (Please ask to be sure this is all right with those for whom you wish to pray.)

Zadkiel: Archangel of Mercy, Forgiveness, Freedom, and Transmutation

Oh, Zadkiel,
Within your light of mercy, I find freedom.
Opening my heart to forgiveness of self and others,
I transcend transgressions.
Transmuting all in violet flame,
I am liberated into love.

Forgiveness Technique

Place yourself within divine protection through prayer, intention, and invocation of the archangels. Call on Creator and on Archangel Zadkiel. Visualize a column or pillar of violet light surrounding you and filling your space. Imagine the violet flame of forgiveness anchoring at your heart and expanding from there throughout your being. Allow yourself to be infused with violet flame.

Next, place the issue (and all related to it) inside a bubble of violet light with the intention that this energetic sphere hold the emotional resonance of the situation/issue/person so that you can remain detached instead of feeling overwhelmed by related emotional baggage.

Ask the Creator, Archangel Zadkiel, and the angels of divine forgiveness to flood the sphere with violet flame to begin to clear the issue, event, or relationship. Direct the violet fire of transmutation through your body, mind, and being and into the issue, experience, or relationship contained within the bubble.

Call on the violet flame angels to expand the cleansing energy of forgiveness to all persons involved, to you in all moments of your entire existence, to all experiences that are relevant, etc. Allow all detritus to be fully consumed with the energy of the violet flame of forgiveness.

If you wish, you may add loving decrees, affirmations, or intention statements to this process. Sound an intonation to fuel your intentions. It does not matter what tone or note (A, B, C, D, etc.) flows from your lips as long as you utter the intonation with love, forgiveness, and mercy as your intention.

As the violet flame continues to burn through your being and through the bubble housing your issue (and all related to it), imprint (through visualizing) the word "forgiveness" written in violet light on your heart and forehead. See it sinking into your mind, flowing through your heart chakra, and merging with your heart, and/or moving over and through your body (specific areas and/or as a whole) to imprint into the fullness of your being. Finally send the word into the bubble that contains your issue or situation. Repeat this process with the word "mercy" and any other words that resonate with your purpose such as "healing," "love," "freedom," etc.

When you feel the process is as complete as you need it to be now, give profound thanks to the Divine and say something like, "I welcome and offer complete forgiveness; I accept for myself and all involved the purest power of divine mercy and forgiveness."

Follow this with an expression of gratitude to the Divine, and then add, "It is done," stated three times.

Acts of Beneficence Aligned with Zadkiel:

1. Work daily on the process of forgiveness. Forgive self and others for events of the day each evening. Meditating with the Light of Spirit, send forgiveness to yourself earlier in your lifetime. Call on the Creator and Archangel Zadkiel and imagine a violet light flowing from above you that washes through your being on all levels, cleansing specific issues from your past or in the present.

2. Create specific prayers or decrees to heal and enlighten the world and free all life from the bondage of anger and hatred. When you begin by calling on Creator and your higher self, often the words flow. (You may use prayers written by others if you prefer, although writing your own will bring a deeper connection to the words.) Speak these prayers from the heart each time you say them. Let love, light, and meaning emanate from every word as you repeat them daily.
3. Imagine that each day you are Creator's hands working in the world around you to bring blessings. Begin each day by setting this intention and saying a prayer to reinforce it. As you move through your day, ask Spirit to guide you as a helper. Acts of kindness done from a loving heart serve the cause of transcendence and enlightenment.

About the Author

Diana Henderson began her professional life working in editing and journalism and then shifted into copywriting and graphic design. In 1994, a debilitating car accident led her onto the path of healing. For many years, she continued to work part time as a graphic designer, copywriter, and editor as she focused much of her life on the healing arts both as a facilitator and as a teacher.

After 20 years, she closed the doors of her Reiki practice and devoted her time to editing and writing. Her efforts as a writer have birthed *Grandfather Poplar*, her first novel, and *Gathering of Angels*, volume one of *The Michael Saga* series. She has written other books that have yet to be published.

Divine guidance led her to establish the Order of Archangel Michael in 2002 and to later begin holding monthly meetings of A Gathering of Angels in 2005. Both groups focused on connecting to the Creator and the angels, living the Light, and honoring the wisdom of the Divine.

Diana lives outside Raleigh, North Carolina, with her husband, their beloved rescue dog, two noisy, cherished parrots, aged 43 and 34, and the beautiful trees that grace their tiny forest. She still enjoys polishing the prose of her editing clients, teaming with her husband in their publishing company, and creating uplifting writing and art.

www.ingramcontent.com/pod-product-compliance
Lightning Source LLC
Chambersburg PA
CBHW070044080526
44586CB00013B/908